adventures in
KNITTING

adventures in
KNITTING

Breaking the rules and creating unique designs

Brenda SHAPEERO

BLANDFORD

A BLANDFORD BOOK

First published in the UK 1991
by Blandford
Villiers House
41/47 Strand
LONDON
WC2N 5JE

Distributed in the United States by Sterling Publishing Co., Inc.
387 Park Avenue South, New York, NY 10016–8810

Distributed in Australia by Capricorn Link (Australia) Pty Ltd
P.O. Box 665, Lane Cove, NSW 2066

British Library Cataloguing in Publication Data
Shapeero, Brenda
   Adventures in Knitting.
   1. Knitting.
   I. Title
   746.432

   ISBN 0–7137–2199–5

Printed and bound in Singapore by Kyodo Printing Co. PTE Ltd

Many thanks to Inox of Westphalia, Germany, for most generously supplying knitting needles, crochet hooks, tatting shuttles and a French-knitting mill; to Jean and Frederick Wright for the use of their conservatory for photography; to Carmel Bowden for testing some of my instructions; to Polly Frenaye-Hutcheson for advice on North American shopping practices; and to the Business Equipment Division of the Minolta Camera Company for helpful advice and assistance concerning the use of my Minolta PCW Word Processor, which made the writing of this book so much easier than it would otherwise have been.

INTRODUCTION

*t*his is a book about experimenting, about using and abusing the rules of knitting to create stimulating designs of your own. It is also about making shopping for yarn an exciting pastime in its own right and about creating exotic garments without having to spend a great deal of money.

Knitting can often be a dull craft, containing little sport. If you are blessed – or cursed! – with the skill, you frequently end up being exploited. Friends and relatives foist patterns on you for dreary cardigans and jumpers that don't interest you in the slightest. Always under the tyranny of the pattern, the yarn is merely a means of building up the garment, like so much ballast, rather than something to give delight.

This is a pity, for today there is an almost overwhelming variety of yarns on the market. Long gone are the days when only 2-, 3- and 4-ply, all in dull, predictable colours, were available. Now yarns come in many different forms – chenille, ribbon, knobbly, whiskery – and they are spun from alpaca, linen, silk, mohair, cashmere – mixtures of all kinds. You can even knit with genuine feathers and artificial fur! And, of course, modern dyes produce a range of the most exciting colours.

The trouble is that you look longingly at such profusion and feel frustrated – either because the most exciting yarns are

too expensive or because they are so tempting you would like to try them all out, and that would mean knitting up dozens of garments for which you couldn't possibly find a need!

However, there is no need to use any particular yarn in large quantities. In fact,

Here are some of the exciting yarns that you can search out cheaply.

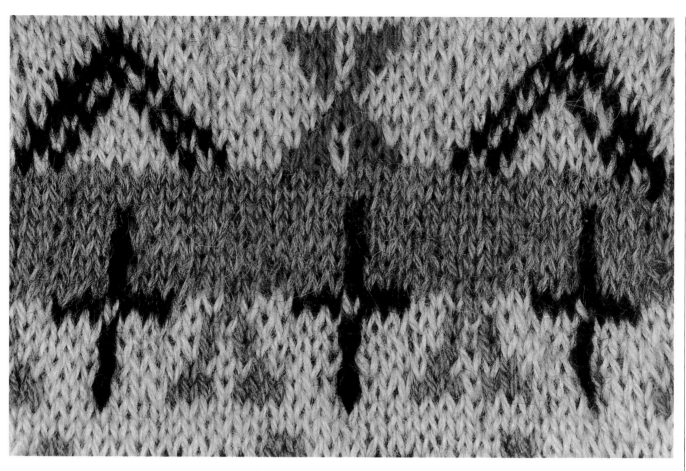

Conventional Fair Isle knitting.

some of the more daring yarns can be too rich when handled in this way and are better bought and used in small amounts. Cultivate the habit of looking around carefully and snapping up discontinued or out-of-season lines at reduced prices. If you do find a special new yarn that you can't resist, buy just an odd ball or two at the full price.

On your yarn-hunting forays buy what is available. Don't set out with a pre-conceived idea of the pattern you're going to work to, but regard yourself as a chef who chooses fresh ingredients on the market, buying what is in season and generating the menu *after* making the purchases.

Combine your leftovers from knitting other garments with your newly acquired odd balls to make exciting and

fresh designs. Become an opportunist, adopting a more freewheeling approach to buying and using yarns. Discard your patterns and transform your knitting from a humdrum, increasingly stale craft into an exhilarating art. And knitting *can* be an art. Just like painting it uses colour for self–expression. Like painting too, knitting can be made to represent in a literal way not only the outward world of landscape, flowers and animals but also the inward world of abstract forms.

Indeed, knitting, with its three-dimensional texture, its discipline of stitches, the dictates of each yarn — How will it hang? How will it link with another? — lends itself best to abstraction. Many of the traditional forms of knitting, such as Aran and Fair Isle, achieve their decorative effects by exploiting stitch and yarn

without recourse to direct pictorial representation.

This book will show you how to put yarns together in unexpected ways by creating experimental samples and then how to incorporate your experiments into whole garments of your own design.

The main object is to encourage you to have fun by inventing designs of your own. Much can be done simply by varying and stretching a limited number of stitches. You will find little in the following pages beyond straightforward stocking stitch (stockinette stitch) and garter stitch, although these are explored at some length. Nor is there a profusion of patterns for complete garments, although, just to show you what can be done, there are a number of patterns for finished articles, such as hats, jumpers

and wall hangings.

These patterns that are included exploit some of the rule-breaking ideas promoted in the book. You may find them rather longer than the patterns you're used to, but this is inevitable as there are constant changes of yarn and stitch, and few repeat rows. Nevertheless, the patterns are simple enough if followed row by row. They are mainly variations on the simplest of knitting stitches, and no special skills are involved.

The idea is to show you what can be done. To get yourself into this mode of knitting, you can copy the patterns in this book but use your own yarns. Nevertheless, as soon as you feel able, I hope that you will start to make your own variations and then go on to create complete designs of your own.

Part of a conventional Aran sweater I knitted up.

THE YARN HUNT

Now here are some suggestions on how to get your hands on some unusual yarns. Start with your local wool shop. Go along with an open mind and without clutching a knitting pattern. Do this regularly and after a while you'll begin to discover yarns you never knew existed. Don't stick to just one outlet but make a point of dropping into other small yarn shops in your area. Shops really do carry different stock. When you are on holiday or on days out, carry on the hunt, looking to see what is available far from your home territory.

Unless you go into one of the really special and exclusive shops, a proportion of the yarns stocked will, of course, be the common lines – humdrum 4-ply (sport) and double knits (worsteds) – but almost every shop you go into will have something different on its shelves. Even the dreariest looking establishment can house some exciting little gems. You will recognize the sort of place – the window with the faded advertisements for wool that is no longer available and the mounds of Cellophane bags of cheap, rather coarse-looking yarns in crude colours.

Nevertheless, to prove the point, it was in just such a place that I once found some of the most beautiful cashmere tucked away. It was an exotic line from Bernat Klein, whose wonderful yarns I greatly admired, although they were normally well beyond my financial resources. Nevertheless, to rid herself of what had clearly been a rash purchase, the shopkeeper sold it to me at a third of the marked price. I have been lucky enough to find such treasures only on rare occasions, but it's all part of the exhilarating pastime of yarn hunting.

Clearance baskets are always a source of excitement, and most shops have one displayed somewhere. Of course, the larger the store, the larger the basket and the greater the choice. Even the exclusive yarn shop usually has one, tucked away in some inconspicuous corner.

Have a good old rummage. Don't be put off by initial disappointment. Sometimes you will find only run-of-the-mill 4-ply (sport) and double knit (worsted) and a bit dusty at that, but these baskets merit more than a cursory glance. For some inexplicable reason the most stimulating yarns tend to bury themselves under a heap of rather dull, uninteresting stuff. There's always the chance of experiencing that thrill as your fingers fall on something different. Good yarns are so often distinguished as much by their texture and feel as by their appeal to the eye.

If the clearance basket fails to come up with something that appeals to you, speak to the shopkeeper. It's surprising what is kept tucked away in the stockroom, and you may be lucky enough to

Watch out for bargain baskets!

track down some extraordinarily good quality yarns by doing this. The proprietor may be so delighted to be relieved of a bag of long-stored oddments that you will be able to buy them at a ludicrously low price.

Adopting these approaches, you will acquire some really unusual and expensive yarns that you might not normally consider buying. Use the exotic yarns as a counterpoint to the more ordinary yarns that can, of course, be bought in this same scavenging way.

You'll soon become oblivious to the occasional bemused look from behind the counter if you go frequently to the same shops and buy only odds and ends!

Department stores often put large quantities of the same yarn in their clearance baskets. Not quite enough to make a complete sweater, which is, of course, why it's being sold off cheaply, but if the yarn is a good one, buy it. (Avoid the temptation of grabbing yarn just because it *is* cheap! We are, after all, aiming at quality!) You can combine it with small quantities of the more exotic yarns in your collection to make a very reasonably priced and exceptional garment.

As with all sales, clearance baskets tend to be stuffed with yarns that are out of harmony with the season. There is a natural reluctance to contemplate thick wool in the fever of a heatwave or insubstantial cotton when the temperature is below freezing. Overcome this aversion and delve in.

Closing-down sales are a source of even cheaper yarns and often in large quantities. Carefully scan the local newspapers, especially the free papers that are constantly being stuffed through our letter-boxes. Every so often you will come across an advertisement for just such an occasion or there may even be a write-up on the shop that is unfortunate enough to be closing down.

These are marvellous opportunities to stock up with large amounts, but *plan* your excursion. Problems can arise when you have to hump your purchases home. You may end up with packages that are far larger than you'd envisaged, which can create real difficulties if you have to travel by public transport. It can be most embarrassing having to attempt to clamber on to a bus, as I once did, with three huge packs of Icelandic wool. Too large to stuff into a shopping bag, they were bursting from the brown paper bag supplied by the shop, and the Cellophane packs were slipping and sliding, threatening to decant themselves into the gutter. It is best to take a friend, or even two, with you if you can.

Of course, closing-down sales present you with a dilemma: the closer to the deadline you wait, the cheaper you'll be able to buy. But then you risk someone else getting there before you. The decision can only be yours!

You can also try discount ware-

Some of the yarns I have tracked down.

houses, which, as the name suggests, are much larger than ordinary yarn shops. The one I most often frequent stretches to two expansive floors, and this provides tremendous scope for finding something really worthwhile. In fact, it was here that I bought as many grubby-looking cones of white cotton as I could carry for the price of an ordinary ball of handknitting wool. From this, used double, I made a man's sweater, a slipover and, used singly, a tablecloth. And I *still* have plenty more in my store cupboard.

A word of warning here. Some manufacturers copy the more exotic varieties of yarn and sell them at a much lower price. These may well find their way into discount warehouses. At first glance they appear more or less identical to the originals, but in fact, if you examine them closely, you'll find the texture coarser and the colour cruder and less vibrant. If you use these yarns, you may find that they drag down the overall quality of your finished garment.

For those fortunate enough to live within reach, there are the shops attached to the mills where yarn is actually pro-

I was able to use cotton/ linen yarn, extravagantly doubled up (since I'd bought it cheaply), to knit this sleeveless slipover.

A cone of very cheap cotton was transformed into a lace tablecloth, with plenty left over.

A few balls of textured cotton, culled from a bargain basket, were all I needed to knit this slipover.

duced. Here, discontinued lines or slightly blemished products are sold to the public at discount prices, but they do tend to be localized in particular manufacturing regions. For example, within the British Isles mills have, since the days of the Industrial Revolution, been concentrated in such traditional manufacturing and sheep-rearing areas as the north of England and southern Scotland.

There may be times when you're looking for a small quantity of special yarn to add spice to your collection and cost is not a priority. If so, watch out for some off-the-beaten-track venues. These can be craft fairs, where people may be spinning and dyeing their own yarns, craft centres, where special exhibitions are held, agricultural shows and other unlikely places –

no doubt you'll discover your own equally useful sources, from which you'll be able to find hand-spun, vegetable-dyed yarn or even yarn spun from dog hair and other unusual animal fibres.

But a question arises. If you are gathering yarns in such a random way and from so many diverse sources, won't your collection be rather chaotic and lacking in any kind of unity? The answer is that people have their own personal taste in colour. This will subconsciously affect your choice when it comes to selecting and buying yarn and produce a spontaneous harmony. As your collection grows, the colours will blend together, almost automatically, into a unique and satisfying combination that reflects your own particular personality.

ODD BALLS

In addition to my trophies from the yarn hunt – my assortment of purposely acquired odd balls – I have accumulated a large stockpile of leftovers from years of making garments. From time to time, like an archaeologist sifting through artefacts for evidence of events long past, I go through this collection. Each ball of cotton or linen or silk has a history. It can be traced back to a garment made a year ago, a decade ago, for an aunt, for a friend, or to a particular day out, an exciting shop far from home. I can almost talk myself out of using a yarn for sentimental reasons! At least this foible demonstrates that yarn is something special, that it is something to be chosen with care, which will, in itself, be a stimulus to design – that it is not something merely to cover the square inches.

I suddenly realized just how many of these odd balls I had when someone asked me to design and make a very large multicoloured cardigan, with lots of coloured patterns. My initial reaction was that it was going to cost a fortune to buy so many different colours for one garment. However, by the time I'd gathered together all my odd balls, I found that, with some judicious purchasing of extra yarn, it need, in fact, cost very little.

In addition to odd balls, you may want larger quantities of yarn to use as a background. If you can't acquire enough of a particular yarn to use right through a piece of knitting, you can always make a virtue out of necessity and split it up by pushing in here and there an unexpectedly different yarn that will lift your design. Make a policy of keeping your designs open ended and the yarns mixed. Then, if you run out of a yarn that cannot be repeated, it doesn't matter. It will be broken up within the garment anyway.

Similarly, don't worry if you can't acquire the amount of a yarn you need from the same dye lot. Just make sure that between the different dye lots you have a few rows of a contrasting yarn as a spacer. This way your background will have more character, with the subliminally changing shades of the same colour mimicking the infinite variety of the imperfections found in nature.

Incidentally, if you do need large quantities, don't overlook the possibility of using yarn on cones designed for knitting machines. This works quite satisfactorily on needles.

The character of the background yarn will depend on you. You may go for stark contrasts in colour – a navy blue background to set off a scattering of red and yellow odd balls, for example – or you may prefer to harmonize colours delicately – a light blue background with soft lilacs and pale pinks. Whatever your preference, the idea is to have plenty of material to offset your special odd balls.

This Brown Striped Jumper was knitted up in a rich variety of yarns using only garter stitch.

Remember, colour is not the only factor. Think of texture and use a background of smooth, plain yarn as a contrast to a richly textured odd ball or mohair as a background studded with a scattering of a tightly woven cotton yarn.

In working at a design such as the one in cotton and mohair illustrated here, it is important to put together a suitable combination of yarns. There are no definite rules, but always bear in mind the thickness and fluffiness of the mohair compared with the tightness of the cotton and consider how the two will go together. If

A delicate cotton was used here to create a pattern on a ground of thick mohair.

achieve the combination that is best for your idea.

The same goes for the use of colour. Subtle contrasts can be effective, but there must be adequate contrast for your design to be discernible. If your mohair and cotton are too alike, the design will simply disappear.

As your collection grows, your box of odd balls will come to include various quantities of, perhaps, mohair, wool, cotton, silk, or mixtures of, for example, silk and mohair, mohair and wool or cotton and linen. There are countless possible combinations to try, all of them stimuli to spark off design ideas. Here is a pattern that uses garter stitch throughout but is made interesting by mixing unusual odd balls with a straightforward background yarn.

BROWN STRIPED JUMPER

The body of the jumper is worked from side to side. The instructions here will fit up to 107cm (42in) bust.

Materials

700g (25oz) assorted chunky (bulky) weight yarns in black (Bl), brown (Br), ginger (G) and red (R); 50g (2oz) mohair (M); a small amount of chunky (bulky) weight fancy knobbly yarn (FK).

there is insufficient contrast between the two yarns, for example, your design will appear a little flat. On the other hand, if the mohair is too fluffy and the cotton too thin, the cotton will tend to disappear and the design will be lost. It is important to keep on experimenting until you

One pair of 6mm (US 10) needles and one pair of 5mm (US 8) needles.

Tension (gauge)

$9\frac{1}{2}$ sts to 10cm (4in approx.) on 6mm (US 10) needles.

Abbreviations

cont = continue; dec = decrease; k = knit; p = purl; st(s) = stitch(es); tog = together.

BACK AND FRONT

(Both alike) Using 6mm (US 10) needles and G, cast on 60 sts and knit 2 rows. Then continue as follows:

K 2 rows M, k 2 rows Br, k 2 rows R, k 4 rows FK, k 2 rows Br, k 2 rows G, k 2 rows M, k 2 rows R, k 2 rows G, k 2 rows Bl, k 4 rows FK, k 2 rows G, k 2 rows Br, k 2 rows M, k 2 rows R, k 2 rows Bl, k 2 rows Br, k 2 rows G, k 2 rows M, k 4 rows FK, k 2 rows Bl, k 2 rows R, k 2 rows Br, k 2 rows G, k 2 rows M, k 2 rows Bl, k 6 rows FK, k 2 rows G, k 2 rows Bl, k 2 rows R, k 3 rows M, k 1 row Br, k 2 rows R, k 1 row Bl, k 3 rows Br, k 2 rows G, k 2 rows FK, k 2 rows M, k 2 rows Bl, k 2 rows R, k 2 rows G, k 2 rows Bl, k 2 rows M, k 2 rows Br.

Cast (bind) off and sew back and front tog, approximately 20cm (8in) in from each side edge, to form the shoulders.

SLEEVES

(Both alike) With 6mm (US 10) needles, pick up 71 sts (35 from each side of shoulder seam plus 1 st in centre). Then work as follows.

K17Br, k2G, k4Br, k3R, k8Br, k3FK, k8Br, k3R, k4Br, k2G, k17Br.

Cont working with the colours as set. **At the same time** dec 1 st at both ends of every 4th row until 45 sts remain.

Change to 5mm (US 8) needles and work in k1, p1 rib as follows.

Work 4 rows Br, 2 rows G, 1 row Bl, 3 rows R, 2 rows Br, 2 rows G, 2 rows Br. Cast (bind) off.

BACK AND FRONT WELTS

(Both alike) Using 5mm (US 8) needles, pick up 60 sts evenly along one lower edge. Work in k1, p1 rib as follows.

Work 3 rows G, 2 rows Br, 2 rows R, 2 rows Bl, 1 row G, 1 row Bl, 1 row Br. Cast (bind) off.

Sew up side and sleeve seams.

NECK

Turn a small amount of knitting to the wrong side of the work and slip stitch in place to form a narrow hem.

As you stockpile your odd balls, don't worry too much about the weight of each particular yarn. You can always put two, or even three, thin strands together if you want to knit with a thicker yarn. It's intriguing to watch colours and textures merge, rather as flavours blend in cooking.

If you are worried about combining several thin strands of yarn, twist a few together to see what effect you get. If this is inconclusive, knit up a few rows. It won't take long to knit a swatch of, say, 20 stitches and about 25 rows, which will give you a very good idea of how the finished fabric will look and feel. You may be surprised by the exciting and unique effects you discover. You can, of course, achieve fascinating results by putting a thick yarn up against the thinnest of yarns, as can be seen in the Icing Sugar Hat.

ICING SUGAR HAT
Materials

100g (4oz) assorted yarns in chenille (CH), cotton (C) and double knit weight (worsted) mohair (M); a small amount of

The Icing Sugar Hat was knitted in stocking stitch (stockinette stitch) and garter stitch, using chenille, cotton, mohair and wispy yarn.

fine, wispy yarn (WY).

One pair of 4mm (US 6) needles.

Tension (gauge)

18 sts to 10cm (4in approx.).

Abbreviations

k = knit; kyfw = keep yarn at front of work; mcfc = match colour for colour; p = purl; rep = repeat; st(s) = stitch(es); st st = stocking stitch (stockinette stitch); tog = together

Cast on 106 sts.

Rows 1–8 Beginning with a knit row, work in st st with CH.

Rows 9–10 St st with WY.

Rows 11–12 St st with CH.

Rows 13–16 St st with M/WY used tog.

Rows 17–18 St st with CH/WY used tog.

Row 19 P3CH, p3M/WY kyfw to end.

Row 20 Knit, reversing colours of previous row.

Rows 21–22 Knit with WY.

Row 23 Knit with M/WY used tog.

Row 24 P1C, p1WY to end.

Row 25 Knit mcfc to end.

Row 26 As row 24.

Row 27 K3WY, k3M kyfw to end.

Row 28 Purl, reversing colours of previous row.

Row 29 K2CH, k2C to end.

Row 30 Purl mcfc to end.

Rows 31–32 Rep last 2 rows.

Row 33 Knit to end with M/WY used tog.

Row 34 Purl to end with M/WY used tog.

Row 35 P5M/WY, k5C kyfw to end.

Row 36 Knit mcfc to end.

Row 37 As row 35.

Rows 38–42 Beginning with a purl row, work in st st using M/WY tog.

Row 43 P4CH, p4M/WY kyfw to end.

Row 44 Knit mcfc to end.

Row 45 Purl mcfc to end.

Row 46 Purl with CH/WY tog.

Row 47 Knit with WY.

Row 48 Purl with WY.

Row 49 Knit with CH.

Row 50 Purl with CH.

Row 51 Purl with CH.

Row 52 Knit with CH.

Row 53 Knit with M/WY used tog.

Row 54 Purl with M/WY used tog.

Row 55 Knit with C/WY used tog. **At the same time**, k2tog every 4th st.

Row 56 Purl with C/WY used tog.

Row 57 With C/WY used tog, k2tog across row.

Row 58 As row 56.

Row 59 As row 57.

Row 60 Draw yarn through remaining sts. Pull up tightly and secure.

Sew up seam with a back stitch. Turn a small amount of fabric to the reverse of your work to form the brim and slip stitch into place. Make a tassle using a combination of your yarns.

The essence of this method of purchasing yarns, and knitting to your own designs, is that you can use your leftovers, together with the odd balls of exciting and normally expensive yarns that you have bought at knock-down prices coupled with bargains of plainer yarns. You may, however, occasionally want to indulge yourself by buying a small quantity at full price to complete your repertoire of colours and textures. After all, it is important to get just the right look and feel throughout your garment – this lapse in strict economy won't add greatly to the overall cost!

Once your palette of yarns is to your satisfaction, you can have marvellous fun putting all the colours and textures together. And you can rest assured, if you knit and design in this way, your sweater, skirt or whatever else you may choose to make will be unique to you.

EQUIPMENT FOR KNITTING

*Y*ou will probably have most of the equipment necessary for the techniques discussed in this book, but to jog your memory there is a checklist below. You should be able to get anything you don't have from a good yarn shop. However, for some things, like circular needles, you may have to go to one of the larger stores. To avoid too much expense at one go, I suggest buying your extra equipment as and when you need it.

NEEDLES

STRAIGHT NEEDLES

Straight needles are most widely used. They come in different lengths, in a large number of diameters, and are sold in pairs.

Metric (mm)		American (US)	
2	_____	0	_____
$2\frac{1}{4}$	_____	1	_____
$2\frac{1}{2}$	_____	–	_____
$2\frac{3}{4}$	_____	2	_____
3	_____	–	_____
$3\frac{1}{4}$	_____	3	_____
$3\frac{1}{2}$	_____	4	_____
$3\frac{3}{4}$	_____	5	_____
4	_____	6	_____
$4\frac{1}{2}$	_____	7	_____
5	_____	8	_____
$5\frac{1}{2}$	_____	9	_____
6	_____	10	_____
$6\frac{1}{2}$	_____	$10\frac{1}{2}$	_____
7	_____	–	_____
$7\frac{1}{2}$	_____	–	_____
8	_____	11	_____
9	_____	13	_____
10	_____	15	_____
12	_____	–	_____

Do be sure to choose the needle length most suitable for your particular project. Nothing is more irritating than having a few forlorn stitches on disproportionately long needles, or too many stitches crammed on to a short needle, obstructing your knitting and threatening to drop off the end of your needle every time you put your work down.

Plastic-coated metal needles or needles made entirely of plastic are most common, but wooden or bamboo needles are being increasingly sold. Despite the attractiveness of these needles made of an organic substance, plastic and metal needles are still more resistant to accidental breakage.

CIRCULAR NEEDLES

Circular needles are very useful in most types of knitting, and they can be used in two ways. You can knit continuously round and round so that there is no need to create seams. This enables you to make a sweater without seams to the armholes or a skirt without side seams.

Alternatively, you can knit conventionally back and forth as you would on straight needles. This is particularly useful if you are making large garments, such as

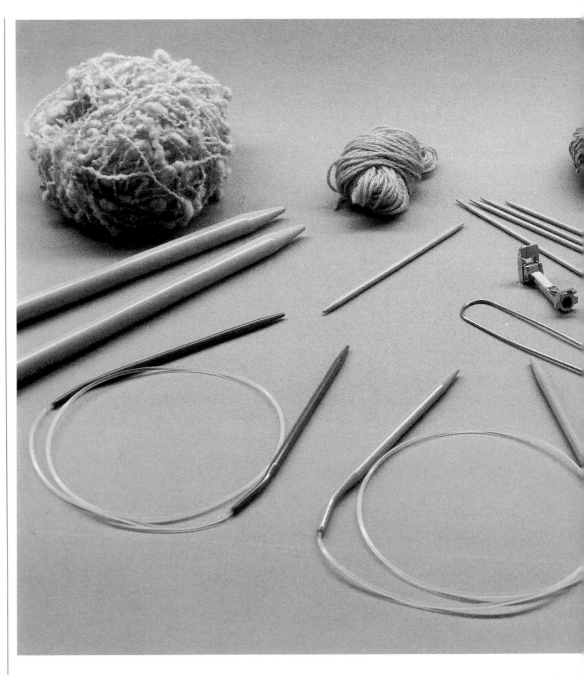

A selection of straight, circular and double-pointed needles, with a cable needle, stitch-holder and sewing-machine foot. And, of course, a cross section of yarns.

shawls, when there are too many stitches to be held conveniently on a straight needle.

Circular needles consist of two short needles joined together by a loop of pliable nylon, on which your stitches lie as you work. Although the loop is thinner than the needles themselves, this does not affect your tension (gauge). A further advantage is that circular needles don't get caught up on the arms of your chair.

You buy them singly, in various lengths and diameters.

DOUBLE-POINTED NEEDLES
Another variation is the double-pointed needle, which, as the name suggests, has a point at each end. Again, these come in various lengths and diameters, but they are sold in sets of four or five. They have

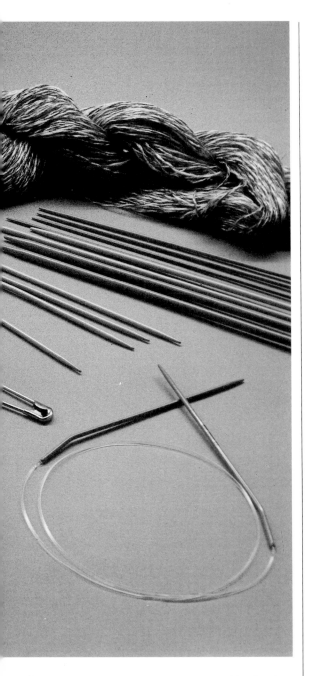

are some of the other items you might need.

CABLE NEEDLES

Cable needles are short and have points at both ends. They are mainly used in specialist work, such as Aran knitting, for holding stitches at the back or front of your work to create a cable.

STITCH-HOLDERS

These resemble enormous safety pins. They are used to hold stitches on one side – of a neck or pocket, for example – while you knit up the other side.

All needles are expensive. If you haven't already got a complete set, buy a pair as and when you need them to help spread the cost.

SEWING NEEDLES

You will need sewing needles to sew up your work and to decorate it with embroidery. For straightforward sewing up you will need a large-eyed, blunt needle, but for embroidery you need one or two sharp-ended ones as well to suit different thicknesses of thread. Arm yourself with a comprehensive collection of varying sizes.

SEWING MACHINES

If you have to sew up a lot of knitwear and it's a task you don't enjoy, a sewing machine can be useful, but you will need a special foot. Knitwear is more flexible than cloth, so this foot is designed so that it doesn't push and distort your material as it moves through the machine. It will save a lot of time and frustration if you press your work before you start sewing with your machine. After this, your seams should be pinned and tacked carefully together. Then you are ready to sew.

an advantage over circular needles in that they can be used with just a few stitches, and this makes them invaluable for small items. Using four or five at a time, you can produce seamless socks and gloves, while sets of longer needles can be used to create the necks and cuffs of garments.

The more you knit, the more you'll find the need for additional equipment. Here

EQUIPMENT FOR DECORATION

*i*n addition to the tools described in the previous chapter, a number of further items might come in handy for decorating your knitting. You will find some of them described in this section, but this is not an exhaustive list. In the larger stores in particular you may come across other items which you will find useful and you may even invent your own. But as far as this book is concerned you will need no more than the following.

Some equipment you might use for decorating your knitting – crochet hooks, tatting shuttles and gadgets for French knitting, both home made and bought.

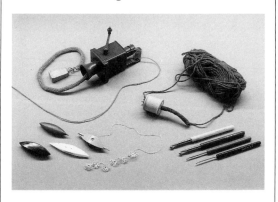

CROCHET HOOKS

Available in various sizes, crochet hooks are particularly useful for trimming the edges of garments. For instance, you may have a neckline that looks rather unfinished but feel that the usual ribbing would be too cumbersome. Here, a simple border of double crochet might be just the thing. Most books on knitting stitches also contain a section on crochet where you will find an adequate description of the required techniques.

Crochet hooks are also very handy for retrieving dropped stitches and pulling knots through to the back of your work.

TATTING SHUTTLE

Tatting is a technique of lace making that can also be employed to make an attractive edging or decoration. Tatting shuttles were traditionally used with a fine crochet hook, but most modern shuttles have a hook attached, which does away with the need for a separate crochet hook. The techniques involved are dealt with in EMBELLISHMENTS.

FRENCH-KNITTING BOBBINS

The technique of French knitting is described in EMBELLISHMENTS. At a price you can obtain purpose-made mills for French knitting. These are very simple and quick to use. In just a few minutes you can have long lengths of tubular knitting. You can achieve the same results by using an old-fashioned, wooden cotton bobbin, and make your own at virtually no cost. To do this you simply hammer four small nails into the top of your wooden cotton reel.

If you can't find an old wooden bobbin, you can use a block of wood, through which you drill a hole. This has the advantage of giving you control over the size of tube you make. But using these hand-made bobbins will take you much longer to produce a finished tube of knitting.

EXTRA EQUIPMENT

*t*here are many items of equipment on the market that you can buy, but be selective – it is so easy to be seduced by advertising or attractive packaging when all you really need is paper and pencil or needle and cotton. Your work basket becomes cluttered with gadgets you never use. So here are a few items that I find useful.

A TAPE MEASURE is an absolute must for all knitters, while a **ROW COUNTER**, although not essential, can be very useful; some types are more expensive and elaborate than others.

You may find the following items useful when designing.

GRAPH PAPER is mainly for use with geometric patterns. It is essential only if you want to work out your design very carefully before you start knitting and if you like to keep a record of what you have done. Normal graph paper is not particularly suitable as in most cases a knitted stitch is wider than it is deep. Now, however, you can get graph paper that is purpose-made for knitters to overcome this problem, and this should be available through art materials or graphic art shops.

A SKETCH BOOK will allow you to keep a record of your design work and to jot down any ideas that may occur to you. You will also need **PENCILS** for drawing out your design – the most useful are 2B, B and HB – and an **ERASER** (the plastic varieties smudge less). Build up a selection of **CRAYONS** and/or **FELT PENS** and/or **PAINTS**. Choose whichever you prefer. Despite their convenience, felt pens and crayons are available in only a limited range of colours, and if you enjoy painting you can mix just the colours you require. Then, of course, you will need a **PALETTE** of some kind – old margarine tubs from the kitchen can be used instead. Saves a lot of money!

Extra equipment for the knitter – pencils, crayons, felt-tip pens, paints, an eraser, specialist graph paper, a tape measure, row counters, sewing needles and scissors.

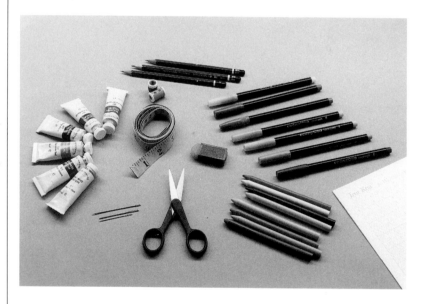

STITCH KNOW-HOW

When you are designing a project you can have fun creating pictures in knitting. These might be literal representations of recognizable subjects such as people or animals or buildings. This is fine, but there is little in the end to distinguish this kind of knitting from painting. The full potential of the craft is not being exploited. As I mentioned earlier, the most satisfying knitting designs take their inspiration from the technique itself. In other words, your designs evolve from the nature of the yarns you choose and from the very stitches with which you put them together.

So let's start with garter stitch and stocking stitch (stockinette stitch). Using these alone, but injecting a few rule-breaking variations, you can achieve really exciting effects.

All the stitches used here are based on those that can readily be found in books of stitches, which you can get from bookshops, newsagents and some yarn shops. Once you are familiar with the stitches, you can begin to experiment with your own versions. Remember, the purpose of this book is to encourage you to discover things for yourself. Always be prepared to break some of the old established rules of knitting.

Here then, in the section that follows, are a few techniques for you to play around with.

BOBBLES

Start by making a basic bobble. First, cast on 12 stitches. Work 4 rows in stocking stitch (stockinette stitch). On the next row k4, then work as follows: k1, p1, k1, p1, k1 into next stitch. Turn. Starting with a purl row, work 5 rows of stocking stitch (stockinette stitch) on these 5 sts. To decrease, using the left-hand needle, take the 2nd, 3rd, 4th and 5th sts over the first st. (Now you're left with just one stitch again.) Knit 4 more sts then work another bobble. Knit the last 4 sts. Purl the next row.

Remember that the first row of your bobble determines whether stocking stitch (stockinette stitch) or reverse stocking stitch is to the front of your work. If you prefer reverse stocking stitch to be on the right side of your work, start the bobble with a knit row after the initial increases.

Once you're happy with this technique you can go on to make variations by extending, shrinking, lengthening, or using different colours, different textures and so on.

TO EXTEND A BOBBLE

Work as for a conventional bobble until the first increase is completed. Turn and purl across these sts.

Next row (of the bobble only) K1, p1 into

Here I formed loops throughout this piece of knitting, which I later decorated, using various types of needle weaving. (For instructions see page 30.)

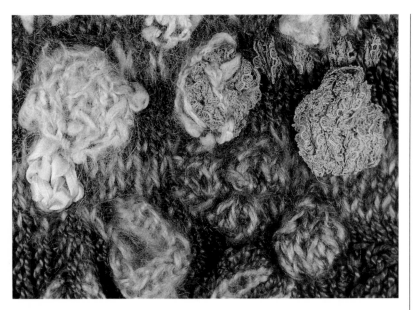

For real extravagance and variety I created these bobbles not only in different shapes and sizes but using all kinds of yarn – silk, cotton, mohair, satin ribbon, cotton ribbon and edging lace.

first st; knit next 3 sts, then k1, p1 into last st (7 sts).

Next row K1, p1 into first st; purl next 5 sts, then k1, p1 into last st (9 sts).

Carry on working in this way until your bobble is the width and length you want. Then, after a purl row, slip all the extra stitches, one by one (starting with the second stitch away from the point of your needle), over the first st until that is the only one you are left with.

TO SHRINK A BOBBLE

K1, p1, k1 into the next stitch on your needle. Turn and, using these 3 sts only, work 2 or 3 rows in stocking stitch.

Cast (bind) off as for the extended bobble. It's quite fun to sprout a small bobble from one of your larger bobbles. Start by following the instructions for an ordinary bobble. Then, when you've worked, say, 3 rows, cast on some extra stitches, but instead of casting them on at the beginning of your bobble, wait until you reach the centre stitch of the bobble you are working on. Increase in this centre stitch, then work this extra sprout. Cast (bind) off the extra stitches and return to your

main bobble. This can be done as many times as you wish.

You can distort a bobble until it is ridiculously long, barely resembling a bobble. Once you have your extra stitches, just keep knitting and turning until it becomes long and loopy. Cast (bind) off as before.

A bobble doesn't need to be confined to one yarn. Try two or more colours. Plain or textured yarns can be used in the same bobble. Vertical stripes or horizontal stripes can be created. Or, perhaps on a large bobble, a textured stitch could be introduced. Then again, perhaps you could make holes in your bobbles.

If you make a lot of bobbles in different textures and pack them close together you will get a really crunchy, luscious finish.

HOLES

A basic hole is made by knitting one stitch, taking the yarn over your needle (to make a stitch), then knitting the next two stitches together. This can be repeated right across the row. These instructions are abbreviated here to k1, yon, k2tog. Knit or purl the next row.

From the basic k1, yon, k2tog you can experiment by varying the size of the hole. Instead of knitting or purling the row after making holes, make yet another row of holes. Scatter the holes at random over your work instead of having them in rigid rows, but make sure that this effect looks intentional rather than accidental.

To make a much larger hole, wrap the yarn around your needle three times. Then knit 4 stitches together. On the return row be sure to k1, p1, k1 into the loops around the needle to make up your stitches again.

Of course, if you want to be really outrageous, you can wrap the yarn around your needle five, six or even seven times. But make sure you knit together the correct number of stitches across the row, so that you end up with the right number of stitches on your needle. This technique may be more suitable for a hanging than for clothing.

If you have a lot of stitches to knit together, try slipping the stitches you need to lose over one stitch (as explained for casting off a bobble). Again, remember to knit into each of the made stitches on the return row.

Holes can be made to sit above each other by repeating the same procedure row after row. However, if you want to stagger your holes, start your next hole row with a knit 2 instead of a knit 1 – for example, k2, yon, k2tog.

RIDGES
You can make a ridge as follows.
Rows 1, 3, 5, 15, 17 and 19 Knit.
Rows 2, 4, 6, 7, 14, 16 and 18 Purl.
Rows 8, 10 and 12 Purl.
Rows 9 and 11 Knit.
Row 13 Fold work at ridge and pick up the first st of row 2 from the back. Knit this st and the first st on the left-hand needle through the back of the loop. Work in this way across the row.

As with bobbles and holes, ridges can be lengthened or shortened or made fatter or thinner. Experiment to see what happens if you don't take them right across the row. Change the colours, change the stitch on the ridge – do anything that occurs to you that will make your ridge look different.

DROPPED STITCHES
Variations on this simple technique are few, but you could try dropping your stitches deliberately and embroidering the threads left behind. Let a stitch drop some way down your work and stop it from going any further by catching it with a sewing needle. Then, on your dropped stitch, embroider a few small stitches with a length of contrasting thread. This will hold the dropped stitch in place and add an extra feature.

An extension of this idea is to drop a number of stitches at intervals and stop them in the same way but at different levels.

A word here about throwing the yarn around your needle two or more times. This technique resembles dropped stitches, but the stitch created in this way gives you greater control. It is always referred to in my patterns as yon.

Different yarns react in different ways to this treatment. A thick, chunky yarn, for instance, will hang quite rigidly even if it has been wrapped around the needle five times or more. Thin cottons when treated in this way, on the other hand, can curl and crinkle. But this needn't worry you, it can add unusual interest. Though sometimes this type of yarn does pull straight later. This will of course depend on the weight of the finished fabric.

Short ridges created in chenille and mohair on a background of textured cotton.

DROPPED-STITCH SAMPLE

Materials

Small amounts of 4-ply (sport) in pale blue mohair (PBM), turquoise cotton (TC), white cotton (WC), white mohair (WM) and white fancy mohair (WFM).

To create a similar piece of work use $3\frac{1}{4}$mm (US 3) needles and cast on 30 sts in TC. Work 3 rows of stocking stitch (stockinette stitch).

Row 4 Using TC, knit, yon twice in every stitch to end of row. Break off TC.
Row 5 Join in WC and knit to end, dropping loops.
Row 6 Knit yon 4 times in every stitch to end of row. Break off WC.
Row 7 Join in TC and knit to end, dropping loops.
Row 8 Using TC, knit.
Row 9 Join in WM and knit yon twice in every stitch to end.
Row 10 Join in WM and knit to end, dropping loops.
Row 11 Using WM, TC and WC tog, knit yon 6 times in every stitch to end.
Row 12 Using WM, TC and WC tog, knit to end, dropping loops. Break off WM and WC.
Rows 13 and 14 Using TC, knit to end.
Rows 15 and 16 Using WFM, knit to end. Break off WFM.
Row 17 Join in WC and knit yon 8 times in every stitch to end.
Row 18 Using WC, knit, dropping loops.
Rows 19 and 20 Using TC, knit to end.
Rows 21 and 22 Using WC and WFM, knit to end.
Row 23 Using TC, knit yon twice in every stitch to end.
Row 24 Using TC, knit yon 4 times in every stitch to end, dropping loops.

Row 25 Using TC, knit to end, dropping loops.

Row 26 Using TC, knit to end.

Row 27 Using WC and PBM tog, knit yon twice in every stitch to end.

Row 28 Using WC and PBM tog, knit yon twice in every stitch to end, dropping loops.

Row 29 Using PBM, knit to end, dropping loops.

Row 30 Using PBM, knit to end.

Row 31 Using WFM, knit to end.

Row 32 Using PBM, knit to end.

Using TC, work in garter stitch for 4 rows. Cast (bind) off loosely.

The knitting is now complete and you have a piece of fabric on which to experiment. Thread a large-eyed, blunt-ended needle with yarn and use this to weave and bind the long stitch loops. Do this with the same yarns used for the knitting. Alternatively, go for yarns that contrast both in colour and texture. On my sample I used the yarns I had knitted with, adding only one extra yarn, a blue cotton ribbon.

To bind the stitches, wind your chosen yarn evenly and tightly around the stitch loops. Executed on a single thread, they tend to curl. But this gives a different effect from winding threads around two or more stitch loops. On these they will be much more rigid. Use buttonhole stitch; it is very effective and is easy to do. Scatter it about your work.

Around some of the stitches I wove my needle in and out of the long stitches, working from the bottom to the top of the stitch loops, until they were all filled in.

For added interest try weaving over three loops only. Then, half-way up, incorporate three more loops to the right. After a few rows working on these

six loops, abandon the ones on the left and work on the right-hand loops only to the end.

Another variation I tried was simply to wind the yarn along the full length of a long stitch and back again. I did this six times or more. The stitch then suddenly pops up from the work, adding another dimension.

I achieved different effects by using different yarns. A mohair looks quite different from a cotton ribbon or a fine silk, but each has its own particular attraction.

We have looked at just a few examples of what can be done to enrich your dropped-stitch work, but plenty more can be explored. So to expand your repertoire further, arm yourself with a good book of embroidery stitches. (See RECOMMENDED READING at the end of this book.)

LOOPING

When you are executing designs that employ more than one colour – Fair Isle, for example – it is usual to carry the threads not in use across the back of your work. Instead, why not try looping your yarns along the front? This allows you to achieve some interesting effects that vary according to the length of the loop and how many rows you work in this manner.

A word of warning however: do not let your loops get too long or they may catch and pull your knitting out of shape. You can, of course, have loops as long as you like, provided you use your sewing needle to couch them down at intervals, as in embroidery.

Loops of yarn kept at the front of the work can completely disguise the actual knitting stitches. In an experimental sample I achieved this pleasing effect very simply. I chose only two different types of

Loops of yarn were draped over the front of my work as I knitted. Afterwards, I picked up these loops and embroidered them.

yarn (two shades of 4-ply (sport) used double, and a fancy knobbly mohair in a similar colour). Working with $3\frac{1}{4}$mm (US 3) needles, I cast on 25 sts and knitted the whole sample in reverse stocking stitch (stockinette stitch) – that is, the purl side is the right side of the finished work.

To begin I worked 7 rows with the 4-ply (sport). On the next row – a purl row – I joined in the mohair. Along this row I alternated the yarns (for example, 4 sts of 4-ply (sport), 5 sts of mohair) to the end of the row. As I worked, I kept the travelling yarns at the front of the work, instead of taking them to the back (as in the pattern for the Icing Sugar Hat). Sometimes I let the yarn stretch over as many as 15 stitches before picking it up

once again to knit. This left long trailing threads scattered over the front of the work. On each row I varied the number of stitches apportioned to each yarn so that more and more of the travelling yarns overlapped and intertwined with each other.

I worked in this way for 20 rows, then broke off the mohair and, using only the 4-ply (sport), worked a further 7 rows in stocking stitch (stockinette stitch).

With the knitting completed, I took a blunt-ended needle and threaded it with the 4-ply (sport). With this I couched down some of the long loops of yarn. In other places, I worked over the loops in buttonhole stitch. Elsewhere I wove the needle backwards and forwards over four strands, shifting after a few centimetres to other strands, but still working over two of the original strands.

I tightly bound some strands along their full length. Others I bunched together by winding the yarn tightly around the long strands, half-way along their length. Shorter strands I left to lie over the knitting.

Then to give my sample a lift, I took just a few small strands of brightly coloured yarn, each no longer than 4cm (1½in), and tucked them behind some of the loops. I sewed these firmly in place on the reverse of the work with a few small stitches, leaving them to peep brightly out here and there. The resulting effect was a soft, but thick, piece of fabric.

To achieve different effects, try using embroidery silks, cottons or any other kind of yarn – thick, thin, plain or textured – instead of the yarn you used for the knitting.

Although the instructions given are for a small sample only, there is no reason why they should not be extended and used to make a thick garment such as a jacket, perhaps with little or no shaping.

A note here: using thick yarn with thin needles causes the cast-on and cast-off (bound-off) edges to curl when stocking stitch (stockinette stitch) is worked. This can be turned to good advantage, as it gives you a ready-made rolled edge.

SLEEVELESS SLIPOVER

Here is a pattern for a sleeveless slipover knitted in a variety of cottons and using just a few of the foregoing stitches. The instructions given here will fit a 92cm (36in) bust.

Materials

350g (12oz) assorted cottons and ribbon yarns in a mixture of 4-ply (sport) and

double knit (worsted); also use any extremely fine fancy yarns that you can obtain. The slipover illustrated was knitted in the following: aquamarine cotton (AC); dark blue cotton (DBC); green cotton ribbon (GCR); Japanese cotton (JC); pink cotton (PC); pink ribbon (PR); silky blue yarn (SBY); silky lavender yarn (SLY); silky pink yarn (SPY); wispy yarn (WY). One pair of 6mm (US 10) needles and one pair of 5mm (US 8) needles; one 5mm

An exotic slipover knitted up in garter stitch and stocking stitch (stockinette stitch), using a number of different types of cotton yarn. (See page 37 for close-up detail.)

(US 8) circular needle or 4 double-pointed needles.

Tension (gauge)
20 sts to 10cm (4in approx.) on 6mm (US 10) needles.

Abbreviations
dec = decrease; k = knit; kyfw = keep yarn at front of work; mb = make bobble; mcfc = match colour for colour; p = purl; rep = repeat; st(s) = stitch(es); yon = yarn over needle.

FRONT PANEL
Using 6mm (US 10) needles and DBC, cast on 60 sts.

Rows 1–2 Knit in DBC.

Row 3 Using DBC, k1, then knit yon twice in every st.

Row 4 Knit to end, dropping loops.

Row 5 Join in PC, k1 with both yarns, then *k1DBC, k1PC, rep from * to last st, k1 with both yarns.

Row 6 As row 5, but purl instead of knit.

Row 7 As row 6, but after 48 sts mb (the instructions for a basic bobble are given on page 27), purl to end.

Row 8 Purl to end. Break off PC.

Row 9 K1 using DBC and PCR tog, then *k1PCR yon twice in every st kyfw, k1DBC yon twice in every st kyfw, rep from * but on st 50 mb as row 7. Then rep from * to last st, k1 with both yarns.

Row 10 Knit mcfc to end, dropping loops. Break off DBC.

Row 11 Join in SPY, k1 with both yarns, then *k1SPY, k1PCR, rep from * to last st, k1 with both yarns.

Row 12 Knit with SPY and PCR, mcfc to end of row. Break of PCR.

Row 13 Knit with SPY yon 3 times in every st. After 44 sts mb, work 2 more sts and mb. Cont to end of row with yon 3 times in every st.

Row 14 Purl with SPY, dropping loops.

Row 15 Join in JC, k1 with both yarns, then *k3JC kyfw, k2SPY kyfw, rep from * to st 43, mb. Work 2 more sts, mb in SPY. Rep from * to last st, k1 with both yarns.

Row 16 Knit mcfc to end.

Row 17 P1 with both yarns, then *p3JC yon 4 times in every st kyfw, p3SPY yon 4 times in every st kyfw, rep from * to last st, p1 with both yarns.

Row 18 Knit mcfc, dropping loops. Break off JC.

Row 19 Purl with SPY, mb in st 50, purl to end.

Row 20 Knit with SPY.

Row 21 Join in SLY and WY, k1 with all three yarns, then *k1SPY yon twice in every st, k1SLY and WY used tog [referred to as SLY/WY from now on], yon twice in every st, rep from * to last st, k1 with all yarns.

Row 22 Knit mcfc, dropping loops.

Row 23 P1 with all yarns, then *p1SLY/WY yon twice in every st, p1SPY yon twice in every st, rep from * to last st, p1 with all yarns.

Row 24 Knit mcfc, dropping loops. Break off SPY.

Row 25 Purl with SLY/WY.

Row 26 Join in SBY, k1 with all yarns, then *k3SLY/WY, k3SBY, rep from * to last st, k1 with all yarns.

Row 27 P1 with all yarns, mcfc and kyfw, purl across row, placing 2 bobbles above previous bobble. On last st, p1 with all yarns.

Row 28 K1 with all yarns, knit to end mcfc to last st, k1 with all yarns.

Row 29 K1 with all yarns, then *k3SBY yon 3 times in every st, k3SLY/WY yon 3 times in every st, rep from * until bobble of previous row is reached, mb in SBY above previous bobble. Rep from * to last st, k1 with all yarns.

Row 30 Knit mcfc, dropping loops. Break off SLY.

Row 31 Join in PCR, p1 with all yarns, then *p2SBY/WY kyfw, p2PCR kyfw, rep from * to last st, p1 with all yarns.

Row 32 K1 with all yarns, then knit mcfc but working 2 more bobbles close to previous bobbles, to last st, p1 with all yarns.

Row 33 K1 with all yarns, then *p2PCR yon twice in every st, p2SBY/WY yon twice in every st, rep from * to last st, k1 with all yarns.

Row 34 Purl mcfc, dropping loops. Break off PCR and WY.

Row 35 Join in AC, p1 with both yarns, then *p4SBY kyfw, p4AC kyfw, rep from * to last st, p1 with both yarns.

Row 36 Knit mcfc to end.

Row 37 Purl mcfc and kyfw to end.

Row 38 Knit mcfc to end.

Row 39 Purl mcfc, yon 3 times in every st kyfw.

Row 40 Knit mcfc, dropping loops. Break off SBY.

Row 41 Join in DBC, p1 with both yarns, then *p1AC kyfw, p1DBC kyfw, rep from * to last st, p1 with both yarns.

Row 42 Knit mcfc to end.

Row 43 P1 with both yarns, then *p3AC yon 5 times in every st, p3DBC yon 5 times in every st, rep from * to last st, p1 with both yarns.

Row 44 Knit mcfc, dropping loops.

Row 45 Purl mcfc and kyfw to end.

Row 46 Knit mcfc. Break off AC at end of row.

Row 47 Join in SPY, p1 with all yarns, then *p3DBC kyfw, p3SPY kyfw, rep from * to last st, p1 with all yarns.

Row 48 Knit mcfc to end.

Row 49 P1 with all yarns, mcfc, purl yon 3 times in every st, kyfw to last st, p1 with all yarns.

Row 50 K1 with all yarns, knit mcfc, dropping loops to last st, k1 with all yarns.

Row 51 Join in SLY, p1 with all yarns, then *p1SPY yon twice in every st kyfw, p1SLY yon twice in every st kyfw, rep from * to last st, p1 with all yarns.

Row 52 Knit mcfc, dropping loops.

Row 53 Purl mcfc and kyfw to end.

Row 54 Knit mcfc to end.

Row 55 K1 with all yarns, then *p3SPY yon 3 times in every st, kyfw, p1SLY yon 3 times in every st kyfw, rep from * to last st, k1 with all yarns.

Row 56 Knit mcfc, dropping loops.

Row 57 K1 with all yarns, then *p1SPY yon 3 times in every st kyfw, p3SLY yon 3 times in every st kyfw, rep from * to last st, k1 with all yarns.

Row 58 Knit mcfc, dropping loops. Break off SPY.

Row 59 Join in JC and WY, p1 with all yarns, then *p1JC kyfw, p1SLY/WY kyfw, rep from * to last st, p1 with all yarns.

Row 60 Knit mcfc to end.

Row 61 Purl mcfc and kyfw to end.

Row 62 Knit mcfc to end.

Row 63 Purl mcfc yon twice in every st, kyfw.

Row 64 Knit mcfc, dropping loops. Break off SLY and JC.

Row 65 Join in GCR and WY and using both yarns tog, purl yon twice in every st to last st, p1 with all yarns.

Row 66 Using the same yarns as row 65, knit, dropping loops.

Row 67 Join in AC/WY, p1 with all yarns, then *p4GCR kyfw, p4AC/WY kyfw, rep from * to last st, p1 with all yarns.

Row 68 Knit mcfc to end.

Row 69 P1 with all yarns, then *p1AC/WY yon 4 times in every st kyfw, p1GCR yon 4 times in every st kyfw, rep from * to last st, p1 with all yarns.

Row 70 Knit mcfc, dropping loops. Break off GCR.

Row 71 Join in DBC, p1 with all yarns, then *p2AC/WY, p2DBC, rep from * to last st, p1 with all yarns.

Row 72 Knit mcfc. Break off AC.

Row 73 Join in SPY, k1 with all yarns, then *k2DBC/WY yon 3 times in every st, k2SPY yon 3 times in every st, rep from * to last st, k1 with all yarns.

Row 74 Knit mcfc, dropping loops.

Row 75 Purl mcfc. Break off WY.

Row 76 K1 with all yarns, then *k3SPY, k3DBC, rep from * to last st, k1 with all yarns.

Row 77 Purl mcfc and kyfw to end.

Row 78 Knit mcfc to end.

Shape neck

Dec at neck edge on every row until 10 sts rem. Keep pattern as follows.

Row 79 K25SPY. Turn, leaving remaining sts on spare needle or stitch-holder.

Row 80 Using SPY, knit to end.

Row 81 Join in SLY, p1 with all yarns, purl kyfw to last st, p1 with all yarns.

Row 82 K2tog, then knit to end, mcfc.

Row 83 As row 81.

Row 84 As row 82.

Row 85 As row 81 but yon twice in every st, kyfw.

Row 86 As row 82, but dropping loops. Break off SPY.

Row 87 Join in JC, p1 with all yarns, then *p3SLY kyfw, p3JC kyfw, rep from * to last st, k1 with all yarns.

Row 88 K2tog, then knit to end, mcfc.

Row 89 P1 with all yarns, then purl, mcfc, yon 3 times in every st to end.

Row 90 K1 with all yarns, then knit mcfc and dropping loops to last st, k1 with all yarns. Break off JC.

Row 91 Join in AC, purl with AC/SLY used tog to end.

Row 92 Knit with AC/SLY used tog to end.

Row 93 As row 91.

Row 94 As row 92.

Cast (bind) off remaining 10 sts. Rejoin yarn to sts on spare needle. Cast (bind) off 10 sts. Work with remaining sts to match first shoulder.

SIDE SECTIONS

Using a 6mm (US 10) needle and AC, pick up 86 sts from one of the long edges.

Row 1 Knit with AC.

Row 2 Join in SBY, p1 with both yarns, then *p4SBY yon 3 times in every st kyfw, p4AC yon 3 times in every st kyfw, rep from * to last st, p1 with both yarns.

Row 3 Knit mcfc, dropping loops. Break off SBY at end of row.

Row 4 Join in GCR/WY, p1 with all yarns, then *P3AC kyfw, p3GCR kyfw, rep from * to last st, p1 with all yarns.

Row 5 K1 with all yarns, then knit to last st, mcfc, k1 with all yarns. Break off AC.

Row 6 Using GCR/WY tog, knit yon twice in every st to end.

Row 7 Join in SLY, k1 with all yarns, then *k2SLY, k2GCR/WY, dropping loops, rep from * to last st, k1 with all yarns.

Row 8 Purl mcfc to end.

Row 9 Knit mcfc to end.

Row 10 As row 9 but yon 4 times in every st to end.

Row 11 As row 10, but dropping loops. At end of row break off all yarns.

Row 12 Join in SPY. Purl to end, dropping loops.

Rows 13–15 Knit.

Row 16 Knit yon twice in every st to end.

Row 17 Join in JC, k1 with both yarns,

then *k2SPY, k2JC, dropping loops, rep from * to last st, k1 with both yarns.

Row 18 Purl mcfc and kyfw to end.

Row 19 K1 with both yarns, then *k1SPY yon twice in every st, k1JC yon twice in every st, rep from * to last st, k1 with both yarns. Break of JC.

Row 20 Purl with SPY, dropping loops. Cast (bind) off.

Work other side to match.

BACK

Work as for front for 85 rows.

Row 86 Work 20 sts then cast (bind) off 1 st at neck edge on every row until 10 sts remain. Leave rest of sts on a spare needle or stitch-holder. Rejoin yarn to remaining sts. Cast (bind) off 20 sts then continue on rem sts and work as for previous neck edge.

Work side panels as for front side panels. Sew back and front of garment together at shoulders and side seams up to armhole (this will be as deep as you choose).

WELT

Using a 5mm (US 8) circular needle and GCR, pick up 174 sts evenly around bottom of garment.

Work in k1, p1 rib, setting colours as follows. On st 13 knit with AC, on st 17 knit with DBC, on st 37 knit with JC, on st 55 knit with SBY, on st 67 knit with SPY, on st 99 knit with SPY, on st 105 knit with DBC, on st 141 knit with DBC, on st 149 knit with SPY, on st 163 knit with SPY, on st 169 knit with AC.

Work in rib for required length, mcfc. Cast (bind) off.

NECK

Using a 5mm (US 8) small circular needle or 4 double-pointed needles and GCR,

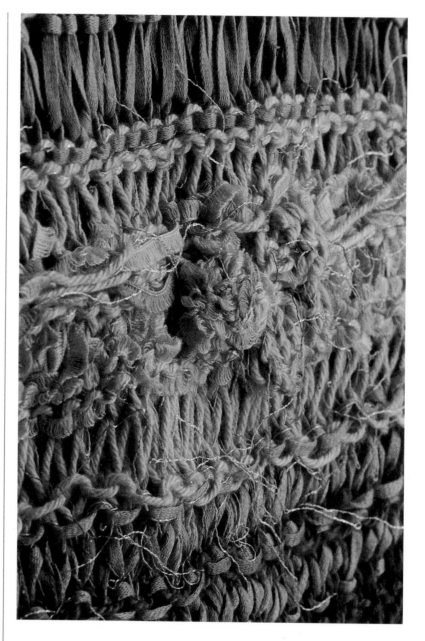

pick up 102 sts evenly.

Work in k1, p1 rib, setting colours as follows. On st 19 knit with SPY, on st 23 knit with SBY, on st 27 knit with JC, on st 31 knit with SPY, on st 69 knit with DBC, on st 75 knit with SPY, on st 77 knit with JC. Repeat for required length. Cast (bind) off.

A detail from the slipover that was knitted in a variety of cottons. This shows how intricate effects can be achieved simply by using garter stitch and stocking stitch (stockinette stitch), but with unusual yarns and by breaking a few basic rules of knitting.

NEEDLE KNOW-HOW

*i*t's worth giving some thought to the size of needle you choose for a project, for herein lies yet more scope for creativity. The size of needle recommended for use with a particular yarn is usually marked on the yarn label, but some specialist yarns from small manufacturers don't always include a suggested needle size, and, of course, yarns from the bargain basket have frequently lost their labels anyway.

Never mind. Continuing in the rule-breaking spirit, here's another opportunity for experiment. For example, if you want to produce a loose, floppy garment, you can knit with larger than recommended needles. Alternatively, you can get a tight feel from the same yarn by using smaller needles. It's surprising what a change there is when you use needles that are just one size apart.

Recommended needle sizes are only a guide. Everyone will produce a slightly different finish to their knitting because knitters vary in how tightly they hold the yarn around the needle as they work.

Moreover, 4-ply (sport) yarn comes in a variety of guises – mohair, cotton and silk, for instance – each of which handles differently. The only way to discover which needle size is best for you is to knit up small *tension (gauge) squares* until you get the right feel for the garment that you have in mind.

I made this bag by sewing together a number of my tension (gauge) squares.

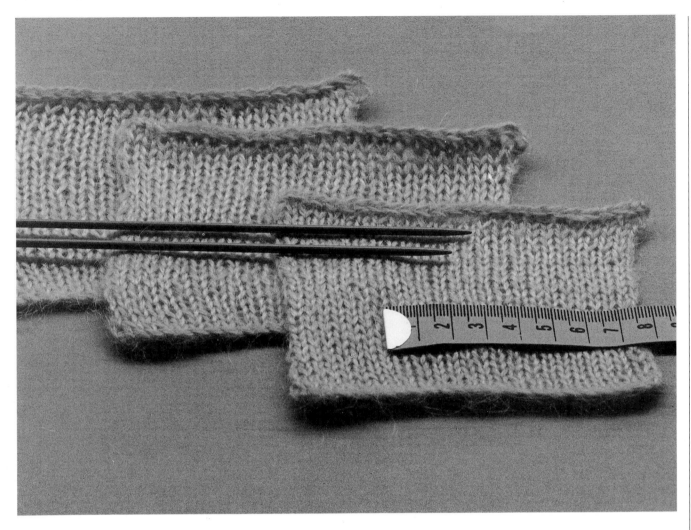

This is what happens when you knit the same number of stitches but change your needle size. These three samples were made using (from to left to right) needle sizes 4mm, 3¾mm and 3¼mm (US 6, US 5, US 3).

Tension (gauge) squares are small pieces of knitting carried out as a test to discover your own personal tension. Cast on perhaps 20 stitches and work about 25 rows in your chosen pattern and yarn. Count the stitches you have to the centimetre (inch) and multiply the number by the width of the fabric you want to produce. This will tell you how many stitches you need to cast on when you start your garment. The number of rows to the centimetre (inch) will tell you how many rows to knit for the required length. You may have to knit up several squares on different sized needles until you get the right feel to your fabric.

When you are surrounded by new and exciting yarns it's tempting to plunge straight in with your needles. But before you do, you must get your tension (gauge) right, especially if you're going to bend the rules. So put aside the time to knit the squares, however tedious it may seem. If you don't, you run the risk of producing a sweater that drops around your ankles or, at the other extreme, one that feels as stiff as a board. One rather excessive way of getting the tension (gauge) right was the technique employed by a friend of mine, who knitted the complete back of a sweater *four times*, on different sized needles, before getting it right!

In the long run, tension (gauge) squares save time, and when you've finished with them, they needn't be wasted. You can put them all together eventually to make a shawl, a bag or a bedcover.

I made this bag from nine squares. Each one had been knitted as an experiment with a different mix of stitches and yarns. I needed to see what tension (gauge) they created and how they would look when knitted up. The squares exploit the stitches and techniques already discussed in this book, and the yarns used range from chunky (bulky) weight to light cotton ribbons and everything in between, including mohair, chenille, double knit (worsted), 3-ply (baby) and even a small amount of dress-lining fabric, torn into strips and knitted in with the other yarns.

There are small bobbles, medium-sized bobbles and one that is quite large, which was made with four yarns knitted together. Then, after I'd created the usual five stitches into the one, extra rows were knitted before casting (binding) off.

Nevertheless, despite these elaborations, the squares were all made using nothing more complicated than garter stitch and stocking stitch (stockinette stitch). Sometimes I wound the yarn over the needle two or more times; sometimes I carried the yarn along the front of the work (as already discussed). There was only one other variation and this was a sample when I formed ridges using stocking stitch (stockinette stitch).

I collected together my completed squares and blocked them separately. I didn't press them, as this would have flattened the bobbles. Once all the edges were straight and uncurled, I used back stitch to sew them all together.

To make the bag, I took a piece of fabric, exactly twice the size of all the squares sewn together. Then I attached the knitting, sewing around the outer edges, to one half of the fabric. Next I folded the fabric double and sewed the side seams together to form the body of my bag. I did the sewing on a machine, using the special foot. It is easier and quicker to use a machine to create a firm stitch, but if you don't have a sewing machine or one of these special feet, all the necessary sewing can be carried out quite securely by hand.

I applied the knitting to one side only, leaving the fabric exposed on the other, but there is no reason why you couldn't have knitting on both faces, using twice the number of tension squares, if you have them.

The shoulder strap was made by crocheting a long chain from yarns left over from the various squares. This needed to be slightly more than three times the length of the finished strap. Only one extra colour was added to give greater interest and lift. Once the crochet was completed I folded the length into three and plaited it, knotting each end for security. The ends of the completed strap were then attached to the bag.

You could make other interesting articles out of your squares. They make fascinating cushion covers, for example, or, if you do a lot of knitting, you could put them to one side until you've amassed sufficient to make a rug to put over your knees or to keep in the car. Or how about a large bedspread? This would be extremely warm as well as unusual.

You may be an uneven knitter – that is, your purl rows may be tighter than your knit rows. This will not necessarily bother many knitters, although to compensate for it in normal knitting, you can

A sample of knitting worked with different sized needles.

work with needles of two different sizes, again using tension squares to discover the best combination for your own personal technique.

Now, this trick can be exploited to achieve deliberately uneven effects. Use exaggeratedly different sized needles together – a very large needle for one row and a fine needle for the next. Switch these around to get a variety of finishes. Perhaps changing the colour or texture of your yarn at the same time as you swop over your needles. Vary the number of rows you do with each combination of needles, and there is no need to stick to two different sizes. Experiment and try three or more on the same piece of knitting.

Incidentally, if you are after really wild effects, you can now buy absolutely huge needles, either singly or in pairs. If on the other hand you are nifty with a knife, you can always try making your own. But be careful of splinters!

COLOUR CONSPIRACY

*n*aturally, in combining yarns some thought must be given to colour. Approach it, as all aspects of creative knitting, with a mixture of daring and discretion. Assuming of course that you're not knitting your finished article all in one colour and shade, you will get your colour effects by mixing different colours or by mixing different shades of the same colour.

If you want a striking effect, go for strong contrasts. Place dark shades up against the palest shade of the same colour. Or, for even greater strength, change the colour at the same time as you change the shade – for example, you could jump from navy blue straight to scarlet in one row.

Alternatively, if you want a subtler, more intriguing effect that does not immediately hit you in the eye, grade your yarns row by row. Move from mysterious shades of navy (is it black, is it blue?) by imperceptible stages, until you're into unambiguous sky blue. Then, of course, you can slip unobtrusively from one colour to another, keeping to similar shades. Naturally you will have to build up a good selection of odd balls before you can grade your yarns in this way. Without being too predictable you do need to maintain overall balance. Use strong colours sparingly. They can hold their own against much larger quantities of quieter colours.

Beware of being seduced. Some yarns look superb when they're on display. I saw some unevenly spun yarn hanging in enticing loose hanks from the wall of a specialist shop. It was space-dyed by hand, and my fingers itched to knit it up into a full garment. However, a completed sweater displayed in the shop window, knitted up entirely in this same yarn, proved to be a disappointment. The effect was too rich and overwhelming.

This type of yarn is best employed with restraint – perhaps a flash here and there against a more subdued background. In fact, I used the yarn in this way for my 'stained glass', dice pattern experiment (see STITCHES, YARNS AND COLOURS). If it were to form part of a whole garment, I would use such a pattern sparingly – maybe a band or two. And there is another advantage from using such an exotic yarn in this way, for the quantity involved is so small that little is added to the overall cost.

You can, of course, use yarn itself as the basis of your colour experiments. One way of creating your own unique colour combination is simply to take two or three strands of different yarns on to your needle and knit them simultaneously.

If in doubt, a bit of experimentation will soon tell you what balance seems right. Again, you can knit test squares to try out your effects. You can also make use of these squares by sewing them together with other test or tension (gauge) squares that may be lying around.

STITCHES, YARNS AND COLOURS

S o yarn texture, thickness and colour, stitch and needle size all contribute to the overall effect of your piece of knitting. Now start to deploy them boldly. Don't worry if all your ideas aren't successful. Be prepared for some disappointments. Nothing exciting or new will come out of timidity.

It may be best to start bending the rules gradually, perhaps by changing colour alone. For example, I knitted up a sample of Aran as an experiment. I kept to the customary stitches, the only departure from convention being that I used three different coloured yarns, instead of the usual natural cream, and when I'd finished, I threaded a random-dyed chunky (bulky) yarn along some of the cables. The effect was quite surprising.

THREE-COLOURED ARAN

Materials

Chunky (bulky) yarns in pink (P), purple (PP) and rust (RT); a length of random-dyed chunky (bulky) yarn.
One pair of 4½mm (US 7) needles and a cable needle.

Abbreviations

k = knit; p = purl; st(s) = stitch(es).
Using 4½mm (US 7) needles, cast on 24 sts (if you want to make a larger sample or even a whole garment, you will need multiples of 18 sts).

Rows 1 and 3 K3PP, k3P, k3RT, k3P, k3RT, k6P, k3PP.
Row 2 and alternate rows Purl, working colours as previous row.
Row 5 K3PP, k3P, *put 3 RT sts on cable needle and leave at front of work, k3P, work 3 sts from cable needle in RT, rep from *, k3P, k3PP.
Row 7 K3PP, k3P, *k3P, k3RT, rep from * to last 6 sts, k3P, k3PP.
Row 9 K3PP, put 3 P sts on cable needle and leave at back of work, k3P, work 3 P sts from cable needle, *put next 3 RT sts on cable needle and leave at back of work, k3P, work 3 RT sts from cable needle, rep from *, k3PP.
Repeat from row 2 for required length.
Then I threaded the random-dyed chunky (bulky) yarn along the cables.

DICE PATTERN

The next step involved changes of yarn texture as well as of colour. From a book of stitches, I took what was described as a dice pattern, which consisted of a repeating pattern of motifs set within an even background. Instead of using a single yarn throughout (as recommended in the book), I used my rich, random-dyed yarn to form the motifs. A change of thickness, texture and colour created the effect of stained-glass windows. By slightly altering the instructions given in the book of stitches, I achieved an intriguingly different end result.

I chose two very different yarns to create this dice pattern – a grey, leather-look cotton to set off a sumptuous red slub, space-dyed wool.

cross 2L [with right needle behind first st, knit second st through the front strand, knit first st in the usual way, then let both sts slip off left needle], p1, rep from * to end.

Row 5 *Cross 2R, k2, cross 2L, rep from * to end.

Row 7 Knit.

Row 9 *Cross 2L, k2, cross 2R, rep from * to end.

Row 11 *P1, cross 2L, cross 2R, p1, rep from * to end.

To achieve the effect illustrated, join in, on row 5, a new colour or texture. Use this for the k2 and repeat on the same stitches on rows 7, 8 and 9. To make the dice longer, row 7 can be repeated many more times.

Here are two more examples of stitches that can be similarly manipulated.

EMBOSSED DROP STITCH

For this you will need multiples of 9 stitches

Row 1 *P4, cross 2R [knit second st on left needle, passing in front of first st, knit first st and slip both sts off left needle], p3, rep from * to end.

Row 2 *K3, p1, lift horizontal thread before next st and purl it, p1, k4, rep from * to end.

Rows 3, 5, 7 and 9 *P4, k3, p3, rep from * to end.

Rows 4, 6 and 8 *K3, p3 k4, rep from * to end.

Row 10 *K3, p1, let next st drop 8 rows down, p1, k4, rep from * to end.

First knit a sample of this pattern just as it has been explained. But, then try making the loops in the centre longer. Make the

For a change, I knitted this Aran sample in three colours. When I'd completed it, I added further richness by threading a lovely extra-thick slub yarn through the cables.

Here is the basic unembellished pattern, which is worked over multiples of 6 stitches.

Row 1 *P2, k2, p2, rep from * to end.

Row 2 and alternate rows Knit the purl sts and purl the knit sts of the previous row.

Row 3 *P1, cross 2R [knit the second st on left needle, passing in front of first st, knit first st and slip both sts off left needle],

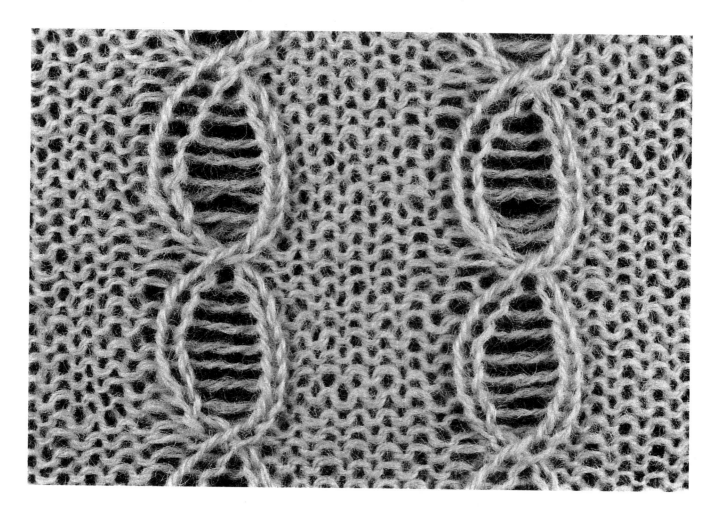

ladders longer. Make them fatter. Use a different yarn for the ladder than for the background. Mix together mohairs and cottons, silks and ribbons and so on.

HYACINTH STITCH

For this you will need to work over a multiple of 6 stitches plus 2.

Row 1 (wrong side of work) K1, *p5tog (k1, p1, k1, p1, k1) into next st, rep from * to last st, k1.

Rows 2 and 4 Purl.

Row 3 K1, *(k1, p1, k1, p1, k1) into next st, p5tog, rep from * to last st, k1.

Row 5 Knit, winding the thread 3 times round needle for each st.

Row 6 Purl, letting extra loops drop off needle.

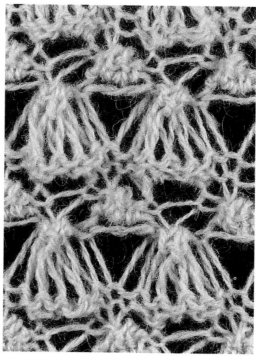

Embossed Drop Stitch worked in 4-ply (sport).

Hyacinth Stitch worked in 4-ply (sport).

Once again, knit a sample of this pattern just as explained. Then try knitting the same pattern with very large needles and fine cotton. Make the small bobbles from mohair and the other part of the pattern in ribbon. Take some edging lace and make the same pattern with that. There are numerous other possibilities once you start experimenting.

Sometimes you can achieve the effect of a change of stitch where in fact there is none. For example, I mixed a simple cotton yarn with a bit of ragged yarn I had made myself by tearing up a length of cotton fabric. The effect was one of great contrast in texture, even though I knitted the whole sample using only stocking stitch (stockinette stitch).

Incidentally, making and knitting up ragged yarn is really fascinating, so the technique is worth exploring a bit. Take a length of material and cut or tear it into strips. Most thin fabrics – silk, lightweight cotton, satin, curtain lining, fine woollen cloth, polyester and so on – are suitable, but make sure that the material you choose is pliable. Stiffer fabrics yield yarns that are difficult to work with and the end result will be unpleasantly rigid and unwieldy.

The width of your strips will determine the thickness of your garment when it is knitted up, the wider the strips, the thicker the garment will be. Your strips can be anything from half a centimetre (about a quarter of an inch) wide. This tearing and cutting method really does give you great variety in your yarn. The process of making the strips can be varied as you go along. If you are cutting the fabric, vary the width by pushing the scissors down a deliberately wavy line, or if you are tearing it, exaggerate the raggedness of your strips.

The texture or weave of the fabric to be cut or torn will also affect the amount of fraying in the yarn you get. Some fabrics will be too loosely woven to be suitable for this particular trick as the yarn they produce will tend to come apart as you knit.

Patterned fabrics can produce delightful surprises. The exciting thing is to watch the random way a pattern is fractured to produce quite new effects when your ragged yarn is finally knitted up. A bold decoration in the fabric will break up differently from a tight, intricate one. But you can never be certain until the whole process, from cutting or tearing to knitting, is complete.

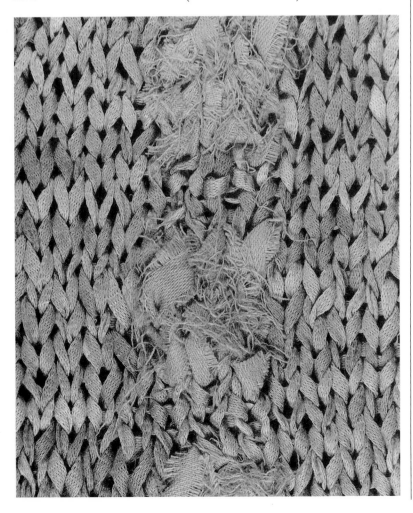

A ragged yarn was created by tearing an old curtain lining into strips. To give an interesting texture, I set this into a simple cotton ribbon. Both yarns were knitted in stocking stitch (stockinette stitch).

When you have made all your strips, you need to knot them together to make a length suitable for knitting. The resulting knots and loose ends can be concealed at the back of your work, or you can make a feature of them by leaving them at the front as part of the design.

When working with ragged yarn – as in other realms of adventurous knitting – the creative use of the wrong needle size enables you to adapt your piece of knitting to the purpose you have in mind. Knitting with small needles and thick yarn produces tight, compact work; large needles and thin yarn produce loose, open work.

Ordinary garter or stocking stitch (stockinette stitch) look very effective when knitted from ragged yarn. From the point of view of diversity stocking stitch has the further advantage that there is a marked difference between the right and wrong sides.

For even more interest, there is no reason you shouldn't use any stitch you want out of a pattern book. However, because of the unpredictability of this ragged yarn technique, perhaps it's best to knit up a sample piece before coming to a final decision.

Ragged yarn can be knitted up into various useful clothes, acccessories or furnishings. Using wide yarn for thickness, you could make a jacket, a coat, a bag or even a rug for the floor, all of which could be lined for greater warmth or hardiness. You could use narrow strips to make a

On the right a portion of Liberty Print fabric; on the left a sample knitted with yarn created by tearing the same fabric into strips.

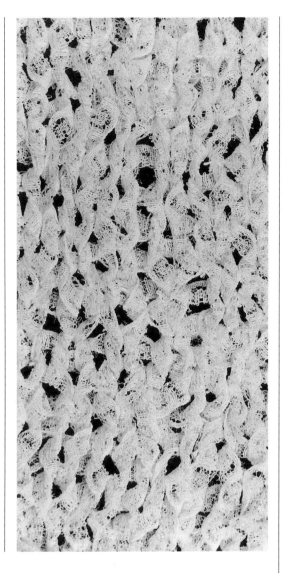

Here's some edging lace knitted up in stocking stitch (stockinette stitch).

Satin ribbon knitted in stocking stitch (stockinette stitch) was attached to a fabric of 4-ply (sport) yarn to make an eye-catching pocket.

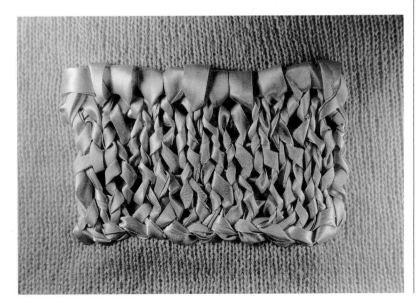

sweater, a hat or even an exotic evening dress.

Another way of obtaining rich textures is to knit with border lace. You can do this by taking a length of narrow lace and knitting it up as it comes. Or wider lace can be cut into strips using a similar approach to making your own ragged yarn from fabric. In this case you would cut your lace down the middle or maybe even divide it into three – a useful ploy since lace is expensive! Though of course lace can frequently be bought cheaply when shops are clearing out their stock.

Needle size again affects the final knitted-up garment. Narrow strips of lace knitted on large needles produce open, frothy work, while wide strips knitted on small needles give a closed, tight fabric. As ever, you must knit up samples to give yourself some idea of what size needles to use.

Border lace can be knitted up to create a striking and rich evening top. All you need do is knit two squares to provide a front and a back, sew up the side seams, then attach the two squares at the shoulders. This could be done with a big bow of ribbon. You could also line the top with satin or silk and finish off the edges with satin ribbon. If you want to be outrageously extravagant, you could even knit a complete evening dress in this way.

For a sumptuously exotic effect, try knitting with satin and velvet ribbons. Enrich your work even further by adding bobbles of various sizes, scattered at random or worked in controlled lines.

KNIT ONE!

When you have mastered the idea of mixing a variety of yarns and stitches, you may still be wondering how to put them all together to make a complete garment. Many expert knitters become worried when confronted with a bag of yarns and no knitting pattern. If an inability to do mathematics is the problem, you can rest assured that only the simplest of calculations are required, and with a basic calculator, they are the work of moments.

In fact, the whole process of making your own patterns is not as difficult as it might at first seem. Assuming you are now in possession of a bag full of irresistible yarns, this is what you do.

1 Decide what you want to make. If this is your first attempt at devising your own pattern, it is best to start with something simple.

2 Equip yourself with a sketchbook. Sheets of paper will do, but it is useful and interesting to keep a careful record of your ideas together in one book and to watch them develop. Gather together your pencils, an eraser, a tape measure and a small calculator.

3 Take your measurements, remembering to allow room for breathing. For instance, if your actual bust measurement is 92cm (36in), make your garment at least 97cm (38in). It is up to you if you want

your sweaters larger. Some people prefer them capacious, others closely fitting.

4 The measurements you need are shown on the drawing.

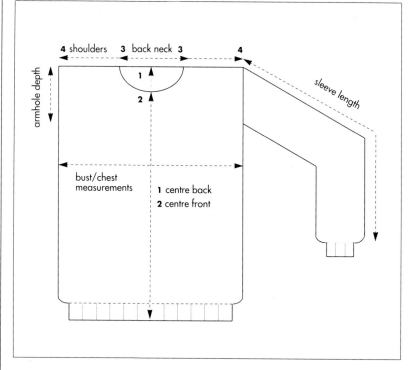

These are the essential measurements needed to create your own basic sweater.

5 With your chosen yarns, knit a tension (gauge) square, 10cm (4in) wide by 10cm (4in) long, using the needle size you feel is appropriate for the yarn that is going to predominate. To begin with it's best to hold your work together by using one particular yarn thickness as a base, but after a while you'll be able to mix thicknesses of yarn with greater flexibility and confidence. Incidentally, if your odd ball has losts its band with the recommended needle size, try it, for a guide, against a

*To work out your own
personal tension (gauge),
place a tape measure over
your sample square and
count the number of stitches
to each 10cm (4in).*

similar yarn that does have instructions. If you don't care for the feel of the fabric when you've done this square, use a different needle size. For example, if the fabric feels too stiff, use larger needles, if it's too loose, use smaller ones.

6 Put the tape measure over your square as illustrated. This will show how many stitches you have to the centimetre (inch). Multiply this number by the width you require; this will tell you how many stitches you need to cast on. Divide this number by two to get an equal number of stitches for the back and front of your gar-

ment. The number of rows to the centimetre (inch) multiplied by the length you require for the finished garment will tell you how many rows to knit.

A square or rectangle will give you a simple shape for your complete garment. If you want to put in sleeves but want to avoid shaping, make these in the form of straightforward rectangles too. If you decide afterwards you would like to draw in the cuff, you can always pick up the stitches at one end and make a knit one, purl one rib.

KNIT ONE PLUS

*a*lthough the special textures and modelling of stitches are the most essential qualities of knitting, you may nevertheless like to consider some two-dimensional design ideas by way of a change from your stitch experiments. So, using small quantities of yarn, here are some thoughts to play around with.

You can start off with simple geometric shapes, such as squares, rectangles, diamonds and triangles, and, as you gain experience, you will be able to plunge straight in and make up your designs as you go along. Working in this way, you can incorporate any small fragment of yarn plucked from your work basket – an enjoyable and successful procedure as long as you keep to a flexible design.

To attempt a more predetermined design, arm yourself with some graph paper. Remember to buy the purpose-made kind that will show you exactly how your design will appear (see EXTRA EQUIPMENT).

If these geometrical motifs are the same colour and are placed at regular intervals throughout your garment, carry the yarn along the back of your work, catching it down with the working yarn (your background colour) every fourth or fifth stitch. If you don't do this, the long strands of yarn at the back of your work will hang loose and tend to catch, so pulling your motifs out of shape.

If, however, your motifs are different colours and are spaced far apart or scattered at random over your work, you should unwind small amounts of yarn from the main ball and knit each motif separately. This will save carrying the yarn over large areas.

Using scraps of yarn plucked from my work basket, I created geometric motifs in stocking stitch (stockinette stitch) to form part of this woollen jumper design.

A few geometric designs set out on special graph paper for you to try. They are based on motifs used in my woollen jumper design pictured left.

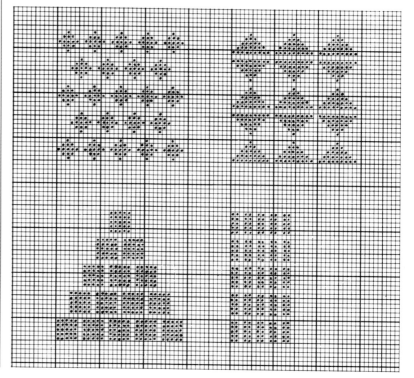

The design for this sleeveless slipover was based on motifs I found in traditional Guatemalan weaving.

Using both these techniques I knitted a sleeveless jumper. This was decorated with stylized motifs based on traditional Guatemalan weaving patterns, that adapt very well for knitting. I developed the design on graph paper before starting work. A large-scale motif, standing on its own, was knitted using separate strands of yarn taken from the main ball. While closely spaced, small motifs were knitted straight from the main balls, the long strands of the working yarn being carried along at the back.

GUATEMALAN-INSPIRED SLEEVELESS JUMPER

The instructions given here will fit a 92cm (36in) bust.

Materials

200g (8oz) 4-ply (sport) in cream (C); small amounts of 4-ply (sport) in brown (B); fawn (F) and rust (R).

One pair of 2¾mm (US 2) needles and one pair of 2mm (US 0) needles.

Tension (gauge)

32 sts and 30 rows to 10cm (4in approx.) on 2¾mm (US 2) needles.

Abbreviations

alt = alternate; beg = begin(ning); cont = continue; dec = decrease; inc = increase; k = knit; p = purl; rem = remaining; RS = right side; st(s) = stitch(es); st st = stocking stitch (stockinette stitch).

The main body of the garment is worked in cream, with some bands of fawn between the designs on the graph paper. Some of the designs from the graph paper will be worked in rust, brown or fawn, or colours of your own choice. You can place the colours as they are shown on the illustration or, if you prefer, mix them around.

BACK

Using 2mm (US 0) needles and cream, cast on 122 sts. Work in st st for 12 rows ending with a purl row. (These 12 rows will be turned to the rear of the work later to make a hem.)

Next row (RS) Purl.

Next row Purl. Cont in st st for another 11 rows.

Change to 2¾mm (US 2) needles and work 12 more rows in st st.

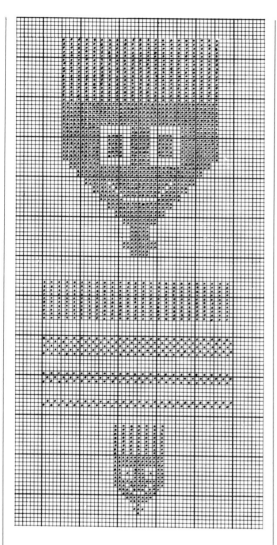

Cont in st st, but follow the strips of pattern on the graph, placing them on your work as and when you require them. (I left bands of cream or fawn between the strips of patterns.)

Work in this way for 43cm (17in), or the required length, ending with a purl row.

Shape armhole

Cast (bind) off 6 sts at both ends of next 2 rows. Cont in st st and, using C as background colour, place the large face in the centre of your work. Follow the design on the graph until the face is completed. Break off R.

Cont in C only and work in st st until the back measures 20cm (8in), or the required

length, from the start of the armhole shaping.

Shape shoulders

Cast (bind) off 11 sts at the beg of the next 6 rows. Put remaining 44 sts on to a stitch-holder.

FRONT

Work as for back until work measures 18cm (7in) from beg of armhole shaping.

Shape neck

Next row K36, turn, leaving rem sts on a spare needle or stitch-holder. Working on these 36 sts only, dec 1 st at neck edge on alt rows until 33 sts remain.

Work in st st on these sts until the garment measures the same as the back at the start of the shoulder shaping.

Cast (bind) off 11 sts at armhole edge on alt rows until all sts have been cast (bound) off.

Keeping 38 sts on the stitch-holder, rejoin yarn to the 36 sts that are left on stitch-holder and work as for right side, but reversing shaping.

Using matching yarn and back stitch, join the front and the back together to create the right shoulder seam.

NECK

Using 2mm (US 0) needles, pick up and knit 134 sts evenly around the neck edge and work in k1, p1 rib for 18 rows. Cast (bind) off loosely.

Join the front and the back together to create the left shoulder seam including the ribbing.

ARMHOLES

Using 2mm (US 0) needles, pick up and knit 130 sts evenly along the edges of the back and the front of your work to form the armholes. Work on these sts in k1, p1 rib for 18 rows. Cast (bind) off loosely. Work other armhole to match.

Sew up side seams. Then fold all ribbing in half and slip stitch to the reverse of your work. Turn the first 12 rows at the bottom of your garment to the reverse of your work and slip stitch in place to create a hem.

Another possibility is to use embroidery to create a design. For instance, I devised a hybrid jumper in which the bulk of the design was created purely from knitting, but a small amount of embroidery was also used. It was a child's picture jumper, and the design consisted of a blackboard with white chalk scribblings. Most of this worked out well in knitting, but a small face posed a problem since it was too thin and tightly curved to be satisfactorily rendered in knitting stitches. To produce the mouth and eyes, as well as the outline, would have required juggling with too many small balls of wool. So I executed this in embroidery using the same white yarn. The design motifs to be executed in knitting were first worked out on graph paper. The face was embroidered on to the finished garment, using only back stitch and French knots (for more on embroidery see EMBELLISHMENTS). The whole pattern is as follows.

A child's jumper with a blackboard design. This was knitted in stocking stitch (stockinette stitch), except for the face, which was embroidered later. (See page 57 for full pattern).

BLACKBOARD JUMPER

The instructions given here will fit up to 70cm (27½in) chest.

Materials

150g (6oz) 4-ply (sport) for the whole garment; a small amount of white mohair. (Allow 100g (4oz) for the body and 50g (2oz) for the sleeves if you choose to knit them in different colours.) The jumper illustrated was knitted in black mohair (BM), red (R) and white mohair (WM).

One pair of 3¼mm (US 3) needles and one pair of 2¾mm (US 2) needles.

Tension (gauge)

24 sts and 32 rows to 10cm (4in approx.) on 3¼mm (US 3) needles.

Abbreviations

cont = continue; dec = decrease; inc = increase; st(s) = stitch(es); st st = stocking stitch (stockinette stitch); tog = together.

FRONT

Using 2¾mm (US 2) needles and BM, cast on 90 sts. Work 4cm (1½in) in k1, p1 rib. Change to 3¼mm (US 3) needles and work 12 rows st st. Cont in st st and keeping BM for the background, join in WM and follow the design from the graph. When the sum is completed break of WM.

Cont in st st and BM and work without shaping until the garment measures 31cm (12in), or length required, from the start of the work.

Shape neck

Cont in st st and BM, work 40 sts. Leave rest of sts on a spare needle or stitch-holder and work on the first set of sts only. K2tog at neck edge on each row until there are 18 sts left on needle. Cast (bind) off.

Return to sts on stitch-holder. Retain the first 10 sts on stitch-holder and rejoin yarn to remaining 40 sts. Work on these

stitches only and complete the left neck edge as for the right.

BACK

Work as for front, following the second graph until both sides are the same length (omitting neck shaping). Cast (bind) off all the stitches straight across the row.

Sew up one shoulder seam.

SLEEVES

Using 3¼mm (US 3) needles and R, pick up 43 sts evenly, starting 15cm (6in) down from the shoulder seam on the front of the work. Then pick up another 43 sts down the back of the work for another 15cm (6in) (86 sts).

Still using R, work in st st to create the sleeve from the shoulder to the wrist.

(This is very useful for young children as the sleeves can be lengthened easily.)

Dec 1 st at both ends of every 6th row until there are 48 sts left on your needle or until the sleeves are the required length. (If the sleeves need to be shorter, decrease evenly across the last row until there are 48 sts; if they need to be longer, dec at both ends of every 8th row instead of every 6th row.)

Cuff

Change to 2¾mm (US 2) needles and work in k1, p1 rib for 4cm (1½in). Cast (bind) off. Work second sleeve to match.

NECK

Using 2¾mm (US 2) needles, pick up 90 sts evenly around the neck. Work in k1, p1 rib for 3cm (1¼in). Cast (bind) off loosely.

EMBROIDERY

Cut a circle from paper and tack it to the front of the jumper. Using it as a guide, with WM and back stitch, embroider around the edge on to the jumper. Remove the paper and work the mouth, again using WM and back stitch. Place the mouth approximately 4 rows of knitting up from the bottom of your circle. Make two eyes, with French knots. Work the back in the same way, giving the mouth an upward or a downward curve depending on whether the sum is correct or incorrect.

Fasten off the WM firmly on the reverse of the jumper with small stitches. Use BM to sew up the side and remaining shoulder seams, and R to sew up sleeve seams.

EMBELLISHMENTS

aving accomplished your overall design, you may want to further enhance it by some form of embellishment. This section suggests a few suitable techniques. Perhaps you may have to put aside a little of your time to make yourself familiar with these additional crafts, but I found that the time was well spent, as many more design vistas were opened up. Instructions for these extra skills can be obtained easily in the numerous books dedicated to particular crafts. (For equipment see EQUIPMENT FOR DECORATION).

TATTING

A craft in its own right, tatting is one way of making lace. It consists of pulling smooth yarn into tight circles and is usually executed with a tatting shuttle and a fine, mercerized crochet cotton that will not stretch.

The origins of tatting lie far back in time, but it reached its modern state of development in the nineteenth century. It has not been a particularly popular craft for some time, which is a pity, for the materials and tools can readily be slipped into a handbag and carried about, to be worked at when you are on a long journey or whenever you find yourself in boring company!

What you do is this: with your tatting shuttle and fine crochet cotton you create rings. At intervals, as you work on your rings, you make picots, which are small loops for decoration and also a means of joining the rings together. For greater flexibility, and to space the rings out, you need to create chains, which are straight lengths of tatting that are used to link rings together. Picots can also be formed on the chains, either for decoration or for attaching other parts of the work to your chain.

The basic technique can be found in any book on tatting, and once you've mastered it, you can use tatting more adventurously.

Tatting used as an edging to give a finished look to a plain piece of knitting.

If you want a chunkier result, work with a thicker yarn, although you may have to put your shuttle aside and work with your fingers only. A word of caution: make sure your yarn is smooth, because rough yarn tends to tangle, split and snap.

The lacy, picot-fringed circles that

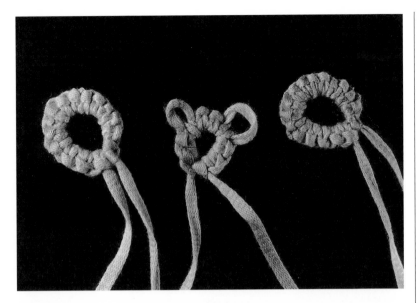

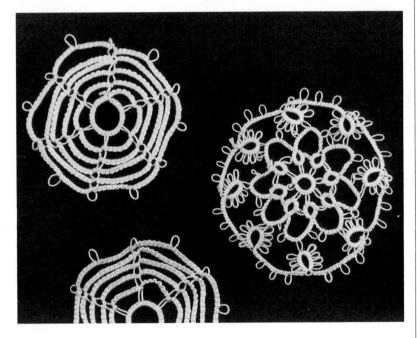

gave just the lift I'd been looking for.

Of course you can vary the size and colour of the rings, or overlap them for a three-dimensional effect. Add as many picots as you want and overlap them, too.

I have only touched on tatting as a means of embellisment, but if you want to pursue the subject further, there are specialist books available. (See RECOMMENDED READING at the end of this book.)

CROCHET

Crochet, like knitting, can be used for creating complete garments, and indeed, it is much quicker than knitting. Here, however, we are simply exploring the technique as a means of embellishment.

Crochet is invaluable for finishing off the edges of garments. A raw knitted edge can often look bald and incomplete, but if you equip yourself with a crochet hook and a book of simple crochet stitches, you will soon discover quick and easy ideas for remedying a bare-looking neck or armhole.

Some basic instructions for adding the simplest of crochet edgings to a garment are described here. Any yarn is suitable for crochet, except perhaps the extremely elaborate bouclés, which tend to catch and snag on the hook when they are pulled through the fabric.

First, take a suitably sized crochet hook – a few experiments will soon show you the best size to use with your chosen yarn – then plunge the hook into a stitch of your cast-on or cast-off (bound-off) edge. Wrapping one turn of yarn around the hook, draw it back through the fabric to make the first stitch. Wrap another turn of yarn round the hook and draw it back through this stitch. Repeat this process, but draw the next turn of the yarn

Top I used my fingers to execute these samples of thick tatting in cotton ribbon.

Above Here are some individual tatted rings that could be used to decorate a plain garment.

tatting produces can enliven a plain garment in a delightful way. I once bought some very fine black cotton, which I knitted up into a classic V-necked, sleeveless slipover. But when I'd finished it, it looked rather severe. Then one evening, as I was rummaging through my box of laces and ribbons, I discovered a length of tatting I'd made some time before. By an extraordinary stroke of luck it fitted the neckline of the slipover perfectly. This

through the two stitches that are now on the hook. This will leave you with one stitch with which to begin the process all over again.

Continue in this way until you have completely encircled an armhole, a neck, a cuff or the bottom of your garment. You have now created a solid band of double crochet, which is ideal for firming up a knitted edge. If, on completion of this first row, you feel greater depth is needed, crochet another row in exactly the same way.

There are many other crochet edgings that you can create. Some are elaborate, but most are simple and effective, and can be found in any book on the subject. (Again, see RECOMMENDED READING.)

FRENCH KNITTING

This is a technique for making tubes that involves winding the yarn around four small nails set into the top of a cotton bobbin (see EQUIPMENT FOR DECORATION), then, with a blunt needle, hooking the stitches that have formed off the nails one at a time. As it grows, pull the work through the centre of the bobbin until it reaches the required length.

The tubes can be used for edging a garment, for three-dimensional decoration, or for making belts and ties. Work produced in this way has a very finished look, and it will not stretch as a narrow band of knitting or crochet tends to do. It does, however, take more time unless you invest in one of the purpose-made machines discussed in EQUIPMENT FOR DECORATION.

MACRAMÉ

Macramé is an attractive technique for knotting and weaving threads or yarns by hand. Like tatting or crochet, it can be used to make a whole garment or a hanging. Unfortunately, it has been debased in recent years by its indiscriminate use in the creation of innumerable bland pot plant holders out of terrible nylon cord! Nevertheless, with good yarn and with some thought and care, sophisticated results can be achieved.

To embellish your knitting, all you need is the mastery of a few basic knots. These can be taken from a specialist book. (See RECOMMENDED READING at the end of this book.)

Macramé is normally worked with purpose-made thread (known as cord in macramé instructions), but almost any yarn can be used. You will be able to experiment with all kinds of yarn, and, of course, this presents a golden opportunity for you to exploit some of your odd balls. Cotton ribbon is ideal, but be cautious with some of the textured yarns, which can be difficult to pull into an even knot. When you come to embellish your garment, you could use the same yarn as the one you have been knitting with. Or go for a contrasting material.

The only extra items of equipment needed for macramé are T-pins to secure the cords ready for working.

Initially, experiment with the easiest of the knots – the half hitch and the flat knot – but once you feel happy with these, you can go on to be more adventurous.

Two ways of exploiting macramé in your designs are described below. In the first, add macramé purely as an embellishment after you have completed your knitting, perhaps letting it hang loose on the garment. In the second method, you make a panel of macramé and incorporate it directly into your knitting.

This macramé panel, attached to a square of knitted mohair, would make an attractive pocket for a jacket.

KNITTED JUMPER WITH MACRAMÉ INSERTION

The back of the garment was knitted in one piece from sleeve edge to sleeve edge, and the front was made in two pieces to take the macramé insertion. The instructions given here will fit up to a 92cm (36in) bust.

Materials

320g (12oz) of 3-ply and a cotton/linen yarn used together; this should knit up to double knit (worsted) weight.
One pair of 3½mm (US 4) needles.

Tension (gauge)

24 sts and 28 rows to 10cm (4in approx.).

Abbreviations

cont = continue; k = knit; p = purl; rem = remaining; st(s) = stitch(es); stst = stocking stitch (stockinette stitch).

BACK

Begin at the sleeve edge and, using 3½mm (US 4) needles, cast on 40 sts. Work straight for 18cm (7in), or required

A knitted jumper with a macramé insertion.

Lace makes an attractive edging to a piece of knitting.

length, in st st. Cast on 54 sts at one side. Cont on these 94 sts for another 50cm (20in). Now cast (bind) off 54 sts and continue on rem 40 sts for another 18cm (7in). Cast (bind) off.

FRONT

Follow instructions as for back but work only 19cm (7½in) instead of 50cm (20in). Cast (bind) off.

Make another piece to match. Press or block the work carefully to straighten the edges.

MACRAMÉ INSERTION

Choose a yarn that slides easily into whatever knot you wish to construct. This particular panel was made up of a number of simple knots, from a book of macramé instructions, and it was executed in cotton ribbon. Since it is almost impossible, in a short space, to write down what I did, the best course is for you to consult a book on macramé and make your own variations.

MAKING UP

Pin the knitting to a flat surface (stiff cardboard or even a firm pillow or cushion will suffice). Pin the macramé piece to the two front edges of the knitting and then tack it firmly into position. Take a sharp needle and sewing cotton and, with small stitches, sew the macramé carefully down. It is most important that the two cast-off (bound-off) edges are kept straight while you work.

If your knots are widely spaced, you can attach a piece of soft lining to the back of your macramé so your garment is not too revealing! Choose a contrasting material to set off the pattern of knots.

In addition to these applications, macramé is also an excellent way of making belts.

RIBBONS AND LACE

Instead of finishing off your work with ribbing or crochet, you can bind the edges with ribbons. This is done by laying the right side of the ribbon on the right side of your knitted edge, and then sewing firmly by hand with back stitch or with a sewing machine. Turn the ribbon over to conceal your sewing. Press, so that the ribbon lies flat, then turn the other half of the ribbon to the wrong side of your work and attach it by hand.

Choose a ribbon to suit the thickness of your finished garment – the thicker your garment, the wider the ribbon needs to be.

Here's an idea for giving a lacy piece of work an even richer effect: just thread satin or velvet ribbons, or lengths of edging lace through the holes after you have finished knitting your work. To secure the ribbon or lace, you need only sew it down at start and finish.

Small items – pockets, collars, cuffs and belts, for example – made in this way take up little material and do much to enhance your work.

KNITTING MACHINES

Although this book is concerned with handknitting, it is worth mentioning briefly the use of a knitting machine. In this context you might regard it simply as an accessory, for there are times when such a machine, if you have one, can be a useful adjunct to your armoury of techniques and equipment for embellishment.

You can, for instance, use a knitting machine to make a belt conveniently and quickly. Cast on a few stitches on the machine, then simply knit until you have the length you want. Alternatively, cast on right along the bed of your knitting machine, knit a few rows and cast (bind) off.

If you are fortunate enough to own a double-bed machine, you will be able to create a tubular length of fabric. This allows you to achieve a result almost identical to French knitting, but in a fraction of the time.

The long strips of knitting, that can be made so quickly by machine, can also be used as decoration and for finishing off the edges of your work.

BUTTONS

Buttons are often regarded as purely functional items, but they can also be seen as part of the decoration you employ to enhance your work. Having taken a great deal of time and care in creating your garment, it is a pity to spoil the overall effect by choosing poor quality, mass-produced buttons. So it is well worth giving some thought to this aspect of completing your garments. Increasingly craftsmen and women are producing an appealing and varied range of buttons, in such materials as porcelain or wood, and these can complement your work beautifully. Watch out for them in discriminating shops, at craft fairs or in mail order advertisements in specialist magazines.

If you want to make your own buttons, this can be done quite simply. One method is to knit a thick bobble in your chosen yarn. Cast on a few stitches, knit as many rows as required, and cast (bind) off. Fold the work over. Sew the two sides and stuff a small amount of kapok through the open end before sewing it up. Now you have your button.

Another way is to use the special kits that enable you to make buttons using a dress-making fabric that complements your yarn. These kits can be bought from most stores and consist of an armature and a base. You simply wrap a soft, wieldy material, such as jersey, cotton or silk, around the armature, which snaps tightly home into the base, which is then attached to the garment.

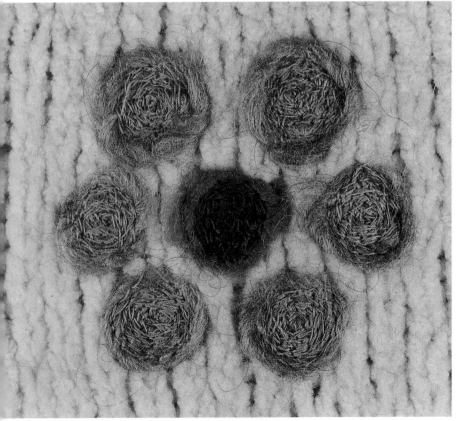

straightforward jumper that needs livening up can be decorated with machine embroidery. If you have a sewing machine, the only additional item of equipment you need is a darning foot, which is used with the feed teeth dropped, so that you can manoeuvre your material with complete freedom.

I tried three experiments on my sewing machine. In each case I used Bonda-web, a fine backing paper, coated with adhesive on one side, which is used by embroiderers. Its normal purpose is to keep fabrics firm while you embroider, but I found by experiment that it could also be used to hold a piece of knitting firm while I embroidered on it.

Place the Bondaweb on the reverse side of the knitting, with the adhesive side in contact with your work. You use an iron, applied directly to the Bondaweb, to fix it in place. *Remember to keep your iron from all contact with your knitting. And remember also to ensure that the glue side is facing your work – otherwise it makes an awful mess of your iron, which takes hours to clean off!* Don't worry if the edges of the Bondaweb don't fuse completely to your knitting. This will enable you to peel it off once the embroidery is complete.

For the first sample I knitted a square

MACHINE EMBROIDERY

in white mohair. Then I lightly outlined my design on the right side of the work, using a felt pen especially made for this purpose as the outline washes out once your work is finished. (These pens can be purchased from good needlework shops.)

In this particular case I chose three shades of pink polyester cotton. I avoided pure cotton as this tends to snap more easily when used for machine embroidery.

I went on to fill in the shapes I had outlined with small stitches on the machine, working back and forth until the shapes were dense with stitches. When I was satisfied with the appearance of my design, I broke off the cotton and peeled away the Bondaweb. This must always be done very carefully, so as not to distort your work.

The second experiment was done in a similar way to the first, but this time the initial sample was knitted in chenille. On to this I then appliquéd small lengths of pink and red yarns, that I had twisted into circles, and attached them to the chenille with pink and red cottons. Using the machine as before, I worked round and round in small circles, removing the Bondaweb when the design was complete.

For my third example I knitted two separate pieces in red and pink chunky yarn. I butted the two pieces together and attached them both to the Bondaweb. I then appliquéd another shade of pink

chunky yarn back and forth across the junction between the two pieces. Again, the Bondaweb was peeled away once the embroidery was finished.

This last technique is a useful and effective device for putting strips of knitted fabric together with something other than straightforward sewing.

Here I joined two pieces of knitting together by couching yarn across them, using machine embroidery.

Opposite above I used machine embroidery to decorate this piece of mohair knitting with half-moon motifs.

Opposite below These circular motifs were machine embroidered on to a background of knitting in chenille yarn.

POTPOURRI
OF PLYS

there are many possibili-ties for adventurous com-binations of yarns. For a richly tangled interplay of textures, mix thick and thin yarns together on the same needles. To give contrasting bands, knit several rows in a thin yarn, then several rows in a thick one. Put together two or three yarns made from different materials – cot-tons, silks, linens, alpaca – or combine dif-ferent types of yarn – knobbly, ribbon, mohair, suede-look... There's no limit once you get started.

Hurling disparate yarns together unexpectedly is one of my favourite ways of working. I'm often sparked off into doing this by something I've seen. The idea for a hanging came to me after a sudden heavy fall of snow. Before the snow came it had rained very heavily, and then, after all the rain and the snow, it froze very hard. A step ladder had been left outside and forgotten, and water and snow had dripped and fallen on it. The steps had formed themselves quite natur-ally into a waterfall, and all this liquid had frozen and was bulging with great lumps of ice, coated with snow.

Unfortunately, at the time, I was unable to photograph it as I hadn't got a suitable film in my camera (perhaps there's a lesson to be learned from this!) and I didn't have time to start painting or sketching. So I wrote a few words in my notebook, describing what I'd observed on the ladder. Later, I examined my cache of yarns and the end result was this hanging.

WALL HANGING

This pattern may look complicated at first glance, but the actual stitches were simple enough. It's mainly a question of changing colours and textures at frequent intervals, and breaking a few standard rules. Most of the yarns I used had been collected hap-hazardly and so, of course, could not now be obtained, making it impossible for you to create an exact copy of what I did. Nevertheless, bearing this in mind, it would be very easy to create a similar hanging that would be unique to yourself. If you do want to follow what I did, I sug-gest that you read the directions through before you start your own piece of knit-ting. This hanging is approximately 68cm (27in) wide and 88cm (35in) long and the fringe is about 50cm (20in) long.

Materials

200g (7oz) 4-ply (sport) in blue cotton ribbon (BCR), blue mohair (BM), cream cotton (CC), cream mohair (CM), mauve fancy mohair (MFM), mauve silk (MS), pink cotton ribbon (PCR), turquoise cotton (TC), white cotton (WC) and white mohair (WM).
One pair of 3¾mm (US 5) needles.

Abbreviations

k = knit; kyfw = keep yarn at front of

This hanging was inspired by rain, snow and ice. (See pages 70, 71 and 73 for close-up details.)

This profusion of bobbles – in glossy silk, crisp cotton ribbon and fuzzy mohair – taken from my hanging was intended to recreate the feel of snow and ice in cold winter light.

work; mb = make a bobble; mcfc = matching colour for colour; p = purl; rep = repeat; stst = stocking stitch (stockinette stitch); WS = wrong side; yon = yarn over needle.

Using 3¾mm (US 5) needles and WC, cast on 124 sts. Knit 2 rows.
Join in MS. *P2WC kyfw, p1MS kyfw, rep from * to end.

Next row Knit, changing WC for CC.
Rep the last 2 rows two more times.
Next row Knit with MS.
Next row Purl with MS.
After these rows place bobbles (see STITCH KNOW-HOW) towards one end of your work. (This will become the upper part of the hanging.) Crowd the bobbles together, crushing them close to one another. Some of my bobbles were constructed with more than one yarn. (Again, see STITCH KNOW-HOW for more details on bobbles.)
Then, still keeping some bobbles butted up close to one another, let others stray over your work. Change the yarn frequently from CC to MS to BCR to WM and back again.
Over the rest of the stitches on the rows continue to knit and purl, kyfw on the appropriate rows. Sometimes, instead of kyfw, work conventionally to alter the texture.
Rep the above instructions until you are happy that the bobbles are forming a good solid texture on your work. Then, as a variation, slip in a row of small holes. These may be difficult to detect, depending on the yarn you choose, but they will change the texture of your work in a subtle way.
Next row *K1, k2tog, yon, rep from * to end.
Purl the next 2 rows.
Next row Knit with MS.
Next row Join in BCR. *K2MS, k2BCR, rep from * to end.
Work another 3 rows in st st, mcfc.
On the next 4 rows keep the MS sts as in the previous rows, but change the st worked with BCR, by placing the right-hand needle into the 2nd st on the left-hand needle. This st is then knitted before

pushing the right-hand needle into the first st. Both sts are then slipped off the needle together. This gives a twist in your stitches to the right.

Next row Purl.

Next row *K3MS kyfw, k3WM kyfw, rep from * to end.

Next row Purl.

Change MS for CC and work 2 more rows in same way as the last 2 rows.

Using CC only, work 2 more rows of holes. This time the 2nd set of holes will not be placed directly over the first, and to achieve this staggered effect knit 1 extra st at the beginning of the row. (After the work was completed, I threaded BCR through these two sets of holes so that it lay diagonally over the fabric.)

On the next 2 rows and using CM, work in reverse st st.

Next row Knit with TC.

Next row Purl with TC.

Still using TC, make another row of holes. (I found that the different yarns made different shaped holes.) Once again, after the work was completed, I threaded ribbon through these holes, this time using PCR.

Next row Purl with TC and use the same yarn to knit the row after that.

Next row *K1TC, k1MS rep from * to end.

Next row Purl, mcfc.

Rep the last 2 rows twice (6 rows in all), alternating sts and keeping the yarn conventionally at the back (WS) of the work. Cont to use MS but change the TC to MFM, and use these last colours to work another 2 rows to match.

Next row *P4MFM kyfw, p4MS kyfw, rep from * to end.

Work 4 more identical rows.

During all of this, intersperse bobbles over the work, using whichever yarn you consider appropriate.

Work 2 more rows mcfc, but keep the travelling yarns at the back of the work.

Break off MS and join in CC. Then, keeping MFM in the same position as on the previous rows, work another row of holes with CC. These will be created over the MS sts.

Then using st st and mcfc, work 3 more rows.

Make another row of holes with CC.

Change to BM and work in st st for another 5 rows.

Purl the next 2 rows with BM.

Next row As you work, dip your needle down 5 rows and pick up the made st. Knit this st together with its matching st of the

These arrow-like shapes were created by picking up threads from 6 rows below the working row. In the hanging this row will appear vertical and not horizontal as shown here.

row in progress. (This will create an arrow-like shape over your work.)

Next row Knit with BM.

Next row Join in WC. *P2WC, p2BM, rep from * to end.

On the next row create more holes with WC.

Next row Purl with WC.

Next row *K3BM, k1WM, rep from * to end.

Next row Purl, mcfc.

A thick slub yarn was used to form a motif against a thin, leather-look cotton. Stocking stitch (stockinette stitch) was used throughout the sample.

Start the first row of the next 8 rows with WC and work in st st. A quarter of the way across the first of these rows, change to CC. On the next row change more sts from WC to CC, using WC less and less until, on the final row, only 6 sts are worked with it.

Scatter very small bobbles over the last 8 rows to give some added texture.

Work another 8 rows as follows: *K2CC, k2MS, rep from * to end.

Rep this row, working in st st mcfc.

Then create a small ridge of fabric by dipping the right-hand needle down 8 rows and picking up the very first st and knitting it together with the st already on your needle. This action is continued right across your row.

Work 4 rows in st st with CC.

Cast (bind) off. Now you have a piece of material with thick sections of bobbles.

I turned my knitted fabric on its side and, taking some lengths of the yarn I had used for the knitting, I attached them to one of the short edges to form a fringe, matching the strands with the yarns I had used for each row.

I made the fringe by first cutting the yarn double the length I wanted for the finished fringe. Then, using a crochet hook, I drew the yarn through the edge of the knitting until I'd created a loop on one side and was left with two loose ends on the other. I slipped these two ends through the loop and pulled them until the loop was tightly drawn to the edge of the fabric.

When the fringe was complete, I decorated the loose strands in as many ways as I could think of: I plaited them, I twisted them together, I braided them.

It is possible to create patterns not only by changing stitch but by changing the thickness or type of yarn. For instance, using only stocking stitch (stockinette stitch), you can form a motif simply by changing yarn at the appropriate place in the row.

Using thin yarn, follow the pattern for creating holes (described in STITCH KNOW-HOW), but instead of using the recommended needles, try a pair several sizes larger. This will create enormous holes through which you can thread bulbous yarn.

Experiment for yourself. Of course, once you do go out on a limb, you can't be sure all your ideas will work out. So knit test squares with your chosen yarns before embarking on a large project.

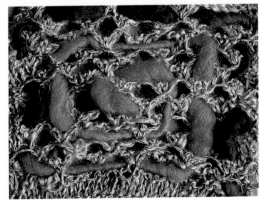

Large holes were created in a sample knitted in thin linen yarn. When the knitting was completed, I threaded a thick, space-dyed, slub yarn in and out of the holes.

A pattern created in stocking stitch (stockinette stitch) by changing from chenille, to silk, to cotton ribbon, to mohair.

Make sure you are happy with the feel of the fabric. Eventually experience will tell you, just by sight alone, what yarns not to put together.

A word of caution: if you use extreme variations of yarn or knit with a large quantity of cotton, your garment may tend to drop. You can get over this problem by knitting your garment from side to side so that the rows in the finished garment run vertically. Then, if knit 1, purl 1 ribs are required, add these later.

STRIPE AND SPOT JUMPER

The instructions given here will loosely fit up to a 107cm (42in) bust. This garment is knitted from side to side so to make the jumper wider, work more rows; to make it longer, add more stitches.

Materials

Main colour (MC): 750g (26oz) chunky (bulky) yarn in beige; contrast colours (CC): 100g (4oz) pale green mohair; 100g (4oz) beige mohair; 50g (2oz) each of red, pink and green cotton ribbon.

One pair of long 4mm (US 6) needles and one pair of long 5mm (US 8) needles; or use appropriate circular needles.

Tension (gauge)

$12\frac{1}{2}$ sts and 11 rows to 10cm (4in approx.)

Abbreviations

dec = decrease; inc = increase; k = knit; p = purl; pw = purlwise; rep = repeat; sl = slip a stitch; st(s) = stitch(es); st st = stocking stitch (stockinette stitch); wb = wool to back of work; wf = wool to front of work.

The following 24 rows form the pattern.

Row 1 Knit with MC.

Row 2 Purl with MC.

Rows 3–4 As rows 1 and 2.

Rows 5–6 Knit with a CC.

Row 7 With MC, *k1, sl1pw, rep from * to last st, k1.

Row 8 With MC, *k2, wf, sl1pw, wb, rep from * to last st, k1.

Rows 9–10 Knit with a CC.

Row 11 With MC, k1, *k1, sl1pw, rep from * to last st, k1.

Row 12 With MC, p2, *keeping wool at front of work sl1pw, p1, rep from * to last st, p1.

Rows 13–18 As rows 1 to 6.

Row 19 With a CC, k2, *sl1pw, k1, rep from * to last st, k1.

Row 20 With a CC, k2, *wf, sl1pw, wb, k1, rep from * to last st, k1.

Rows 21–22 As rows 9 and 10.

Row 23 With a CC, *k1, sl1pw, rep from * to last st, k1.

Row 24 With a CC, *p1, keeping wool at front sl1pw, rep from * to last st, p1.

BACK

Using 5mm (US 8) needles, cast on 75 sts and work in given pattern for 60cm (23½in), or desired length. Note: after working 24cm (9½in) place a marker at one end of your work, then, after another 22cm (8½in), put in another marker; these two markers denote the neck. Cast (bind) off loosely.

To obtain more colour and texture in your garment omit the bands of st st and change one yarn for another more frequently. For added texture a row of purl stitches can replace a row of knit stitches.

This Stripe and Spot Jumper was knitted in wool, cotton ribbon and fancy mohair.

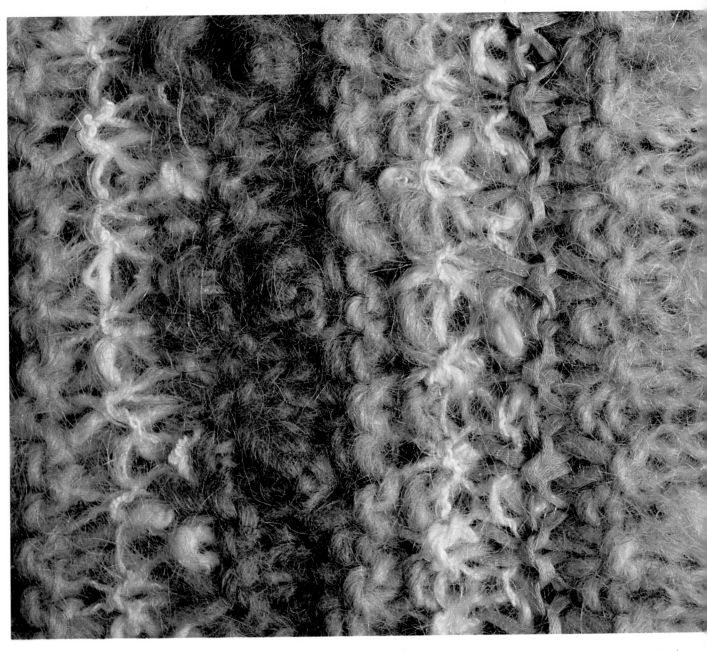

Even more texture can be obtained by placing lines of bobbles between the bands of slipped stitches. Spread these evenly over a band of st st.

FRONT

Work as for back until you have completed 24cm (9½in) or reached your first marker.

Shape neck

Dec 1 st at neck edge on next 10 rows. Work 8 rows on remaining 65 sts.
Inc 1 st at neck edge on next 10 rows. Then continue in your pattern for another 24cm

(9½in) or required length. Cast (bind) off. Sew up one shoulder seam.

NECK

Using 4mm (US 6) needles and MC, pick up 62 sts evenly around the neck edge. Work in k1, p1 rib as follows.

Every purl st is created in MC, but every knit st is worked in one of the contrasting colours. This will give you a rib of stripes. Work in this way for 10 rows. Then cast (bind) off evenly and loosely. Note: it is easier to work if you make small balls of each of your colours so that they don't

reduce the stitches to 32, dec evenly across the last row.

Change to 4mm (US 6) needles and work 12 rows in k1, p1 rib to match the neck. Work the other sleeve to match.

WELT

Using 4mm (US 6) needles, pick up 66 sts evenly from the lower edge of the back. Work 14 rows in k1, p1 rib to match the neck and the sleeve ribs.

Sew up side seams.

Finish off the neck by taking a length of cotton ribbon threaded through a blunt-ended needle. Embroider with this on to one of the side edges of the ribbing, then work the other side edge to match. On one of these edges make two loops for buttonholes. Then sew on two buttons.

You may prefer to dispense with a rib. One way to do this would be to knit a strip of fabric in garter stitch long enough to fit around the bottom of the jumper. Use needles two sizes smaller than those you used to knit the main part of the jumper. The rows would run in the same direction as those in the main body of the garment. Then sew this strip to the bottom of the jumper to form the welt.

Alternatively, the stitches could be picked up from the bottom of the garment, and using garter stitch, a welt knitted for the depth required. The same techniques could be used to finish off the sleeves and the neck.

Just a suggestion: when you are working cuffs in cotton yarn and want them to fit closely, use knit 1, purl 1 rib and work in this way for 15–18cm (6–7in). Then they will cling to your wrist more tightly.

Though all your experiments may not work out, it's surprising just how many yarns can successfully be combined.

A close-up detail from my Stripe and Spot Jumper, showing the mingling of cotton ribbons and mohairs against plain wool.

tangle at the back as you knit.
Sew up the other shoulder seam.

SLEEVES

Using 5mm (US 8) needles and MC, pick up 37 sts from the cast-off (bound-off) edge of the side of the garment, plus another 37 sts from the cast-on edge. Pick up an extra stitch at the shoulder seam. Work on these 75 sts in the given pattern (or your own variation) but dec at each end of every 4th row until there are 32 sts left on the needle. If you need shorter sleeves, stop working earlier. Then, to

SOURCES OF
INSPIRATION

deas for original stitch designs, motifs, devices for embellishment and so on may occur to you as you handle lengths of yarn, the colours and textures of the material being sufficient to get you going. However, there are times when you may need the stimulus of sources beyond the yarns themselves.

There are many things in the world around us that can form jumping-off points for our imaginations. Naturally, as a knitter, you will mainly be looking for shapes, colours and textures. However your inspiration may not come merely from some specific shape or colour, but also from the feel or atmosphere of an object or a special place – the way a cold winter light falls on the frost-covered berries of a tree, for example.

A special scene may move you so much that you are driven to capture its essence. A musician or a poet might translate this atmosphere into his or her own particular language, just as Mendelssohn did in his overture *Fingal's Cave* or Wordsworth did in his poem *Daffodils*. So, in the same spirit, the knitter may capture this special atmosphere in yarn.

Bearing this in mind, here are a few suggestions that you may find helpful in your search for different sources of inspiration when you come to create your own designs.

BOOKS

Illustrated books are a natural quarry to be mined. Within their covers I find an endless variety of shapes and colours that lend themselves to interpretation through the medium of knitting. Natural history books are particularly useful. For colour, there is the sheen of a bird's plumage, the luminosity of a flower, the subdued brooding tones of mosses or lichens, and for shape there are the innumerable patterns to be found in plant and animal structures.

There are, of course, many books on traditional crafts, ranging from those on smocking or knitting patterns from pre-industrial Europe to the art and architecture of exotic cultures all over the world. You might be inspired by the applied decoration on the mud walls of an African hut, the decorative effects achieved by the Maoris in the woven bamboo walls of their houses in New Zealand or the wonderful stylized animals that form the basis of so many patterns on garments from Central and South America.

GLACIER HANGING

This piece of work was not inspired by anything visual, but by a passage in a novel that I was reading. There was a vivid description of a glacier that stirred my imagination. My idea was to capture the sense of ice moving remorselessly through a mountain valley. So the next time I went

I was inspired to make this Glacier Hanging by a description in a novel of ice moving across a mountainside.

to my treasure chest of yarns I searched out white cotton, white mohair, white wispy yarn and white/blue/pink wispy yarn – all the colours and textures that evoked snow, ice, mountains and extreme cold.

The white cotton had been left over from a sweater made some summers ago. Other yarns had been hunted down cheaply and were awaiting the right piece of work in which to take their place. The wispy yarn was being almost given away in a large department store. I supplemented these yarns with two balls of cream mohair, which I had, of course, bought at discount price!

To give myself plenty of room, I chose to knit with a large-sized circular needle.

I include here a description of how I made the hanging so that you could make your own version. But there is no reason you should follow exactly what I did. The description is intended only as a guide, and you could easily incorporate ideas of your own.

I used approximately 200g (7oz) of yarn. Some of this was 4-ply (sport) weight, some of double knit (worsted) weight and some was an extremely fine wispy yarn, almost resembling sewing cotton.

Using a 6mm (US 10) circular needle, I started by casting on 100 sts with white cotton 4-ply (worsted). From then on I used only knit and purl stitches. I wrapped the yarn around the needle once, twice –

These faces, taken from my slipover (see page 54), were derived from traditional Guatemalan woven patterns.

up to 10 times a stitch all the way across a row – allowing the loops that had been created to drop below the needle on the next row. Between these rows of huge stitches I knitted or purled normal rows to create a denser look. Sometimes I used one yarn; sometimes two or even three at the same time.

I used white wispy yarn and cream mohair together. I added to these the blue/white/pink wispy yarn and, at intervals, I put the white wispy with the white mohair. Occasionally I used all of these yarns on one row. At times two stitches would be knitted in one colour/texture and two or even three stitches in another. And I repeated these changes of colour and texture right across the row. My aim was to find as many variations as I could, so although the finished hanging looks complex, nothing more was used than knit and purl stitches.

When the hanging was a satisfying length, I cast (bound) off firmly with one of the mohair yarns.

The joy of constructing hangings, as opposed to garments for everyday wear, is that there are very few constraints on your creative powers. They can be quite impractical and outrageous – there is no need to worry about long threads catching on rings or hooking around fingers – and the fact that you can see right through your work is no problem. Whether you feel that a lining behind the hanging will enhance it is up to you. If you decide on a backing, choose a fabric that will blend with the colours in your knitting. Alternatively, you could go for a complete contrast in both colour and texture.

To give the hanging a more finished look, I attached a fringe to the cast-off (bound-off) edge. Somehow that seemed

to work better than putting it along the cast-on edge of the knitting. A fringe consumes a lot of yarn, so make sure that you have plenty left from your knitting. Alternatively, you could select a contrast.

Once the fringe was attached, I decorated it using a variety of techniques, including buttonhole stitches, plaiting strands together, wrapping wispy yarn round mohair strands and simply knotting other sections of yarn together. The wrapped and embroidered strands sometimes twist and turn, but this adds even more interest and richness.

At times it is difficult to predict the outcome of a piece of knitting like this, but this is what is so exciting about adventurous knitting. With practice you will discover more or less how a yarn is likely to react to the way it is handled. But there are always some surprises waiting.

To keep your hanging clean, place it in a pillowcase and wash it in your washing machine with your wool wash items. When it is dry shake it out, making sure the fringe is unravelled. If the mohair seems at all flat, fluff it out with one of the purpose-made brushes that can be bought in most good wool shops or department stores, or you can use a natural teasel. I use one of these, stolen on a late autumn day from the countryside. But if you do this, do make sure that the small creeping and crawling creatures that may have taken up residence in it have been evicted before you take it home, lest they colonize your cupboard!

SCAVENGING

Form the habit of collecting any objects that are likely to fire you with ideas in a fallow moment. Look out for anything that has interesting tactile qualities or

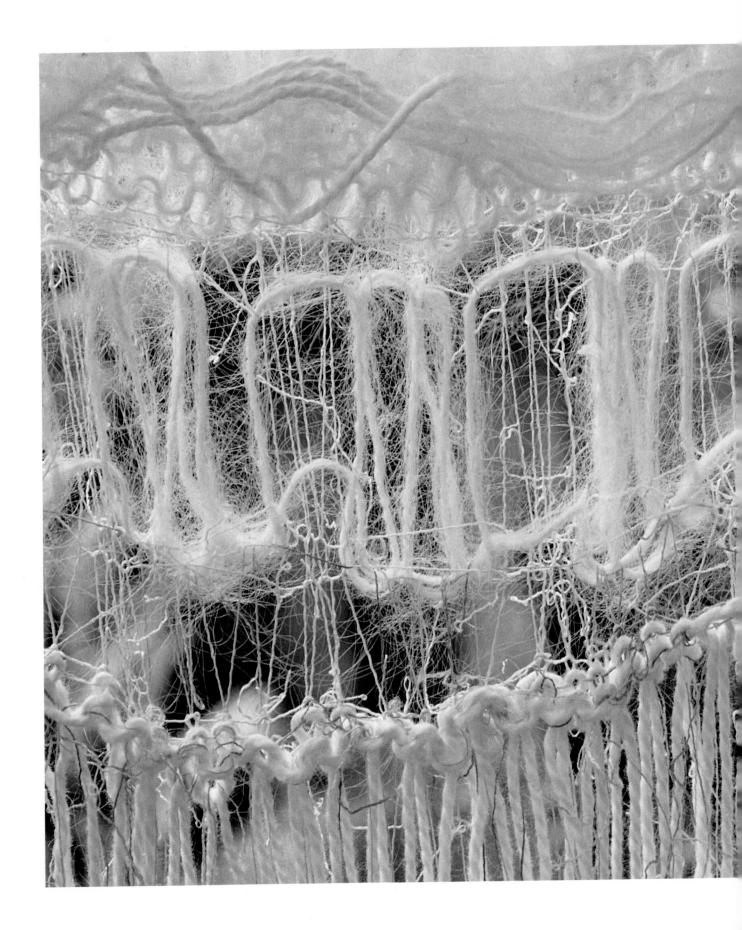

appealing colours: fir cones, flowers (dried or alive), pebbles, postcards, seaweed, even fruit and vegetables from your own kitchen... whatever catches your eye.

MUSEUMS AND EXHIBITIONS

These are always worth visiting. Any type of exhibition could be useful to you; even those that have no apparent relevance to knitting may provide you with stimulating material. For example, an exhibition devoted to rope-making might provide you with some absorbing patterns. Again, trawl whatever new design ideas you can from these sources. The catalogues that accompany these exhibitions are frequently worth collecting as a permanent reminder of what interested you.

SHOPS

Visit shops that sell ethnic clothes, ornamental items and so on. Look at their colours and patterns and maybe poach ideas for shaping your garments.

THE BUILT ENVIRONMENT

Get used to looking closely at the man-made features that make up so much of our surroundings. Decorations on buildings, chance patterns on walls – created by weathering or differences in the colour of bricks and stones – tiles on roofs, chimney pots, pavements, fractured reflections in windows, stained glass all offer shapes and colours to fire the imagination.

THE NATURAL ENVIRONMENT

Apart from providing a storehouse of interesting objects to scavenge, nature is

A close-up detail from my Glacier Hanging (see page 79 for complete work). This effect was achieved using stocking stitch (stockinette stitch) and garter stitch, and by wrapping the yarn around the needle many times and putting unlikely yarns side by side.

an inexhaustible and ever-changing source of colour, shape and texture – the colour of the sky or the sea; the foliage of trees and hedgerows through the seasons; the changing fields, from dark brown furrows of earth to rich golden corn, peppered with bright red poppies; a bank of moss and fern oozing with water; a thick blanket of snow, suddenly transforming a familiar landscape; icicles tumbling from a blocked gutter . . . And here is a pattern for a hat inspired by the colours of autumn.

AUTUMNAL HAT

The instructions here will fit an average size head quite loosely. The hat illustrated was made in a mixture of wools and cottons.

Materials

120g (5oz) of yarns in double knit (worsted) thickness in pink textured cotton (PTC), purple textured yarn (PTY), rust (R) and yellow mohair (YM). One pair of 3¾mm (US 5) needles and one pair of 4½mm (US 7) needles.

Tension (gauge)

20 sts to 10cm (4in approx.) on 4½mm (US 7) needles.

Abbreviations

cont = continue; dec = decrease; inc = increase/increasing; k = knit; kyfw = keep yarn at front of work; mcfc = match colour for colour; p = purl; rep = repeat; st st = stocking stitch (stockinette stitch); yon = yarn over needle.

Using 3¾mm (US 5) needles and R, cast on 100 sts. Work in k1, p1 rib as follows: 2 rows YM, 4 rows R, 2 rows PTC, 6 rows R, 1 row PTC, 1 row YM, 2 rows R. Change to 4½mm (US 7) needles and knit with R, inc evenly across the next row until there are 120 stitches.

Work 4 rows in reverse st st, starting with a purl row.

Place colours as follows: *p2R kyfw, p2YM kyfw, rep from * to end. On the next 3 rows mcfc.

Next row Join in PTC and work 2 rows st st.

Place colours as follows: *p3R kyfw, p1PTC kyfw, rep from * to end.

For the next 7 rows work in st st, keeping the yarn at the back of the work as in conventional knitting, mcfc.

Cont in st st for another 3 rows but join in YM, placing colours as follows: *k1R, k1PTC, k1R, k1YM, rep from * to end.

Next 2 rows Work in st st, mcfc. Break off YM and R. Work 2 more rows in st st.

Next row With PTY, purl yon twice in every stitch to end. Break off PTY.

Next row Knit with R, dropping loops. For the next 6 rows work in reverse st st, kyfw on purl rows. Place colours as follows: *3R, 3YM, 3PTC, rep from * to end. The next 2 rows were worked as the previous 2, but this time the travelling yarns were kept at the rear of the work.

Next row *P1PTY, p1YM, rep from * to end.

Next row *K1PTY, k1YM, rep from * to end.

Next row *P2PTY, p1R, rep from * to end.

Next row With PTY, purl to end.

Next row With YM, purl to end.

Next row *K3PTC yon twice, k3YM yon twice, rep from * to end.

Next row *P3YM dropping loops, p3PTC dropping loops, rep from * to end.

Next row (decrease) K2tog every 8th stitch, **at the same time** placing colours as follows: *k1R, k1PTC, rep from * to end.

A striking pattern on a Victorian garden wall.

I caught this rowan tree in autumn, just when the berries had newly formed and while the leaves were in various stages of decay, giving a wide range of hues.

Next row Purl, using PTC instead of R and R instead of PTC, to end.

Next row K2tog every 6th stitch with PTY.

Next row With PTY, purl to end.

Next 4 rows *P1R kyfw, p1YM kyfw, rep from * to end.

Next row With PTC, purl to end.

Next row With PTC, knit to end.

Next row *P2PTC kyfw, p2R kyfw, rep from * to end. **At the same time** p2tog every 4th st.

Next row *K2PTC, k2R, rep from * to end.

Next row *P2R kyfw, p2YM kyfw, rep from * to end.

Next row Purl mcfc.

Next row Knit with PTC, dec in every st across the row. Break off all yarns.

Thread a yarn through the remaining stitches. Draw these tightly together and secure the thread firmly to the wrong side of the work with a blunt-ended sewing needle. Sew up the back seam.

The above instructions are intended as a guide only, as, once again, the yarns used in the Autumnal Hat were collected cheaply and randomly from bargain baskets.

Try the pattern with your own selection of colours and vary the amount of yarns that travel across the front of the work. You might prefer to use more colours, or perhaps, fewer. Just one word of caution: cotton does not give as wool does, so beware of pulling too tightly any cotton yarns that you loop across your work.

PHOTOGRAPHS

You will probably want some form of permanent record of transitory visual experiences. People who are proficient with a pencil or a paintbrush have an invaluable means of storing a fleeting impression or combination of colours. However, many people are not so skilled or may find the process too cumbersome, in which case it is a good idea to carry a camera whenever possible. Black and white photographs sometimes reveal pattern more graphically than colour, but on the whole colour is the more generally useful medium.

Colour slides are more vibrant than prints, but they are less convenient because of the need for some kind of magnification or projection. So a collection of colour prints, which can be readily referred to and can be viewed together rather than one at a time, is the most useful for your purposes. But try to use fairly slow film (100 ISO), as this gives better colour reproduction and records detail more sharply.

There is no need to have an elaborate camera. A polaroid or a compact 35mm camera will record much of what you see around you. However, if you want to catch large detail at a distance or small detail close up, it does help to have a telephoto or close-up (macro) lens at your disposal. For this you need a single lens reflex (SLR) camera that has the facility to accept a variety of interchangeable lenses.

If you want to pursue the possibilities of photography, there are, of course, innumerable specialist books and magazines on photographic techniques and equipment.

My Autumnal Hat was inspired by seasonal colours.

*t*his is an area that can so easily let a beautifully knitted garment down. You've spent so long creating a sweater or cardigan and you can't wait to wear it – and be complimented on your work! But haste at this stage can be your garment's undoing. So here are a few sound ways to make up your work.

BACK STITCH

This stitch is suitable for sewing up most woollen garments and is most often used. It gives a firm, strong edge.

Place the pieces of fabric to be sewn together with the right sides facing each other. Matching your knitting row for row, insert a blunt-ended needle into the work and secure the thread with a few small stitches. Push the needle to the back of the work. Let it emerge at the front a few millimetres further on. Now take your needle once again to the back of the work at the point at which you previously pushed it to the back. Repeat this procedure until your seam is completed.

Keep the stitches even and not pulled too tightly. The ideal seam should be worked 6mm ($\frac{1}{4}$in) from the edge of the knitting.

If your work consists mainly of chunky yarns, back stitch can make the seams rather bulky, but even with such yarns it is useful for shoulder seams where some rigidity is required.

EDGE-TO-EDGE SEAMS

Place the edges to be seamed close together and side by side. With a matching thread and keeping the rows even, sew the edges up row by row. Carefully done, this technique is useful for sewing up ribbing and chunky fabrics, but it will not give an especially neat finish with finer material.

LADDER STITCH

This is an invisible method of seaming. Once again you need a blunt-ended needle and matching thread. With the right side of your work facing you, pick up a horizontal bar (perhaps half a stitch into your work) and pull the yarn loosely through. Repeat this on the opposite edge of your piece of fabric. Work in this way for a few stitches. Then pull your working thread firmly and evenly up to close the work. You'll find the sewing stitches disappear into your knitting.

This method is less bulky than back stitch, and it has the advantage that, as you sew, you can see what is happening on the crucial right side of your work.

GRAFTING

This is yet another way of putting together two pieces of knitting. The idea here is to make your joins invisible, by eliminating seams – it is particularly useful for shoulders.

When you graft your work together,

MAKING UP

your stitches are not cast (bound) off. First, press the edge stitches carefully to stop them unravelling and curling. To make your work easier to handle, put a row of back stitch through the stitches of the last but one row. (These will be removed once the work is completed.) Then thread a blunt-ended needle with plenty of matching yarn; you will need three or four times the length of the row.

For ease of working, keep your knitting flat. One good way is to pin both pieces of fabric to a cushion. Then continue as follows:

1 Lay the stitches to face each other.
2 Push the sewing needle up through the first lower loop.
3 Take the needle from the front to the back of the first upper loop.
4 From the back of the work push your needle to the front of the second upper loop.
5 Now take your needle down into the first lower loop. Push it through to the back and then bring it forward through the second lower loop.
6 Continue in this way across all the stitches to the end of the row, making sure that all your made stitches have an even tension (gauge).

If you're nervous about letting the stitches off your knitting needle to start grafting, keep them on. Make sure that the points of your needles are lying in the same direction. Then, as you work, manoeuvre the sewing needle around your knitting needle. Now you can let the stitches slip from your knitting needle, one by one, as their safety is assured.

If the idea of grafting worries you, practise on two small samples of stocking stitch. Once you've mastered the technique, you'll find it well worth the trouble. The end result is most pleasing and your join will be completely undetectable.

SLIP STITCH

Slip stitch is used mainly for securing hems. There are two ways in which you can approach it.

In the first method you cast (bind) off your stitches before sewing. With the wrong side of your knitting facing you, turn up a hem. Secure the yarn in your blunt-ended needle to the hem with two or three small stitches, then insert this needle into the main body of the garment, moving from right to left. Lightly pick up one thread only of a stitch and draw the yarn through loosely.

Move along the fabric to the left. Insert the needle into the hem and pick up a thread. Again, pull the yarn through. These two movements will join the hem to the main body of the garment. Just continue in this way until the hem is completely secured. Fasten off.

The second method is carried out

exactly as above, except that you don't cast (bind) off your stitches before sewing. In this instance you take your stitches straight from the knitting needle, one at a time, as you go.

When you use slip stitch, it is easy to keep your hem straight, as all you do is follow your line of knitting. And if you use a matching yarn, you will not see the stitches on the right side of your work.

CROCHET

A suitable crochet stitch for making up would be a simple chain stitch, and all you need for this is a crochet hook and matching yarn. Put the right sides of your work together and secure the seams along the edges with your crochet stitch.

If you prefer to make a feature of the making up, then put your work together with the wrong sides facing each other. Then work your chain stitch with either a matching or a contrasting yarn on the right side of your work. (See EMBELLISH-MENTS, for more detailed crochet instructions.)

SEWING MACHINES

You can, of course, use a sewing machine for making up your work, but you do need a special foot. (For more details on this see EQUIPMENT FOR KNITTING.)

CARING FOR YOUR WORK

*t*here are various ways of taking care of your work, but it is most important you select the best for your garment. Your precious work can so easily be ruined at this stage. In a moment of absent-mindedness, for example, I popped a sweater I'd made for myself, in a beautiful wool and linen yarn, into my washing machine along with my ordinary cotton coloureds. To my dismay I discovered it had shrunk to a third of its original size. So, to avoid a similar disaster, here are a few suggestions.

WASHING

If you have acquired a good proportion of your odd balls from bargain baskets, they will probably be a little dusty, in which case you will want to wash your garment as soon as it has been knitted up.

As you will be using many different yarns together in one piece of work, it's best if you can keep together all your labels from each yarn used so that you can wash according to the instructions for the most delicate of the yarns. In other words, if you have several yarns that are suitable for machine washing, but one that must be hand-washed, you must, unfortunately, wash the whole garment by hand.

Of course, you may have some yarns in your collection that did not have labels when you purchased them. If this is the case, treat them as if they were pure wool and, for safety, always wash them by hand.

To wash by hand, immerse your work in lukewarm water with a suitable detergent. Rinse thoroughly, again using lukewarm water. Ease the water out, without squeezing too hard. Then place the garment in the shortest-spin section of your washing machine. After this, lay the work flat to finish drying. If you have a tumble dryer, you could finish the drying process in that. Here are some important points to watch.

1 *Never* hang your work up when it is wet. The weight of the water will pull it completely out of shape and then it will be ruined.

2 *Never* have the water more than hand-hot. Water hotter than this will matt any pure wool or mohair. And once it has matted there is no remedy.

3 It is important also, when washing, to remember that wool does not like sudden changes of temperature. These can cause your garment to shrink, felt or matt. So always ensure an even temperature is maintained throughout the washing of your garment. If you wash your work in lukewarm water, then always rinse your work in lukewarm water.

A particularly large garment can become impossibly heavy to handle once it becomes waterlogged. Instead of hand-washing, you could have it dry cleaned.

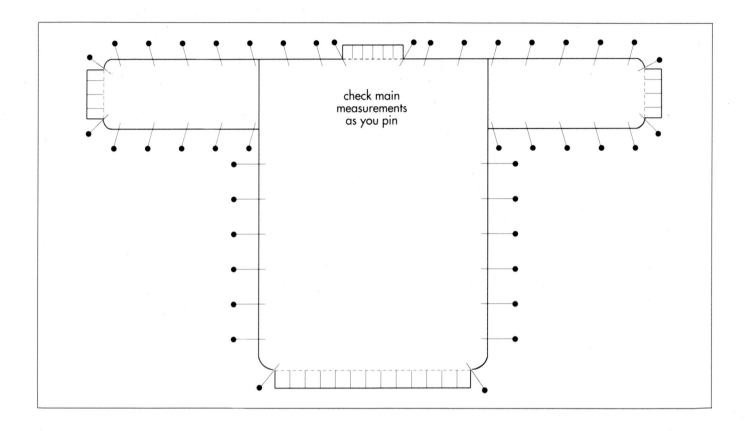

check main
measurements
as you pin

A garment blocked to its
correct size with pins.

BLOCKING

If you've worked with pristine yarns and kept your garment clean – by wrapping it in a tea towel, for example – there'll be no need to wash it immediately. To make sure the garment is in shape, to unfurl the edges, and to get rid of those inevitable crinkles and wrinkles blocking is the answer.

You will need a suitable flat area, such as a firm table. Purpose-made blocking boards, with square grids to make accurate pinning out easier, are available, but anything the right size will do, even the floor. If necessary, protect your surface with a folded blanket. Spread your garment onto this, taking care not to pull your knitting out of shape, which is easily done. Use a tape measure to ensure that it's evenly spread. Smooth out your garment carefully, checking the measure-ments as you go. Secure it to your backing with stainless steel pins (non-stainless will rust and leave marks), placing the pins at short intervals.

Once you're happy that all measure-ments are correct, spray your work with fine jets of cold water, using a spray that you'd use for your indoor plants. Make sure the garment is evenly damp all over.

Don't be tempted to touch it now for at least 24 hours. (If you live in a dusty area, you may want to lay a light cloth over it.)

If you block your work, there's no need to iron or press it. However, you may find blocking too time consuming, or it may be difficult for you to clear enough space to leave a large garment spread out flat for any length of time. If this is the case, you will have to press your work with an iron.

PRESSING

Great caution here. Abuse with an over-hot iron can ruin hours of work. Once stitches have been flattened, distorted or made shiny with heat, there is no way to bring them back to life. So never use your iron as if you were, say, pressing a cotton skirt or a blouse. Be much more gentle.

Take a cloth – a tea towel would be ideal – and soak it in cold water. Place the cloth over your knitting and put the warm iron on to the cloth for a few seconds. Then, when you move to the next position, lift the iron, don't push it along. Pushing will distort your fabric.

Using the odd ball approach to knitting, you may well have a wide variety of different yarns in one piece of work. So read the labels on every ball of yarn. If you have doubts at all about how any particular yarn will stand up to ironing, it's best to stick to blocking. The materials to look out for are acrylic or nylon, which can easily be damaged by ironing. Or knobbly yarns, which can lose their wonderful bubbly texture under the weight of an iron.

Of course, if you have no label to tell you what a particular yarn is made of, it's best to block your work. Then you will have no worries about your work pulling out of shape.

Andes, Eugene, **Practical Macramé**, Studio Vista, 1971

Brittain, Judy, **Step-by-Step Encyclopaedia of Needlecraft**, Ebury Press, 1979

Deuss, Krystina, **Indian Costumes from Guatemala**, Catalogue of Exhibition, 1981

Eaton, Jan, **The Complete Stitch Encyclopedia**, Ward Lock, 1989

Findley and Blandford, **Macramé Projects**, Batsford

Fini, M. S., **The Weavers of Ancient Peru**, Catalogue of Exhibition, 1985

Klein, Bernat, **Eye for Colour**, B. Klein, 1965

The Knitting Dictionary, Mon Tricot

Thomas, Mary, **Book of Knitting Patterns**, Hodder & Stoughton (reprinted 1985)

Thomas, Mary, **Knitting**, Hodder & Stoughton (reprinted 1985)

Thomas, Mary, **Dictionary of Embroidery Stitches**, Hodder & Stoughton, 1934 (reprinted 1989)

Walker Phillips, Mary, **Creative Knitting**, Van Nostrand Reinhold, 1971 (reprinted by Tejedoras Fiber Arts US in 1987)